The Motivated School

Alan McLean

Los Angeles • London • New Delhi • Singapore

First published 2003. Reprinted 2008

 SAGE Publications Ltd
1 Oliver's Yard
55 City Road
London EC1Y 1SP

SAGE Publications Inc
2455 Teller Road
Thousand Oaks
California 91320

SAGE Publications India Pvt. Ltd
B 1/I 1 Mohan Cooperative Industrial Area
Mathura Road, New Delhi 110 044
India

SAGE Publications Asia-Pacific Pte Ltd
33 Pekin Street #02-01
Far East Square
Singapore 048763

Library of Congress Control Number: 2003102874

A catalogue record for this book is available from the British Library

ISBN 978-0-7619-4384-6 (hbk)
ISBN 978-0-7619-4385-3 (pbk)

Typeset by Dorwyn Ltd, Rowlands Castle, Hants
Printed in Great Britain by Cpod, Trowbridge, Wiltshire
Printed on paper from sustainable resources

The Motivated School

Contents

List of Diagrams

List of Tables

About the Author

Alan McLean is a principal psychologist in Glasgow City Council, Scotland's largest education authority. He has taught in a secondary school and a special school for students with emotional and behavioural problems. He is the author of the staff development programmes *Promoting Positive Behaviour in the Primary School, Promoting Positive Behaviour in the Secondary School* and the award-winning *Bullyproofing Our School.* These programmes have been used in schools throughout Scotland over the last ten years. He was seconded for two years as the first National Coordinator of the Professional Development Initiative for Psychological Services. He has served on government advisory groups on bullying, truancy, discipline and social competence. He had a weekly column in *The Scotsman* for several years and is a regular contributor to the *Times Educational Supplement Scotland*. He is currently seconded to lead Glasgow's POLO Programme, (portfolio of optimal learning opportunities) a strategy to reduce disengagement from learning. He has been running training courses for the last four years on Motivating Learning.

Acknowledgements

This book would not have been possible without the support, advice and constant encouragement of many people. I am grateful to school practitioners Heather Hamilton, Headteacher, and Kate Whiteley, Senior Teacher of Lumphinans Community Primary, and Christine Wilson, Headteacher, Langside Primary, for making sure the themes were relevant to the practical school context. Bob Cook, Education Officer, West Dunbarton, and Derek Goldman, Lecturer, Open University gave encouraging feedback on early drafts. Colleagues Ellen Moran, Elaine Miller, Tricia Murray, Angela Jeffreys and Kate Watson from the psychological service read and advised on early drafts. The team at Learning Unlimited, particularly Ian Smith, was helpful in developing the motivation model. Finally I am grateful to Margaret Sutherland and Chris Smith, from the Centre for Support for Learning, Glasgow University, whose constructive criticism was significant in helping to transform the early drafts into a textbook.

This book is dedicated to Michael and Euan McLean

Preface

This book argues that the most powerful motivation for learning comes from inside. The search for higher achievement from governments is pressing teachers to try to motivate students from the outside by threat of punishment or promise of reward. This book suggests that a more effective alternative is to motivate from the inside by using students' positive states to draw them into learning. The best form of motivation is self-motivation. Students, however, need teachers and other staff to help them achieve this state. This book explores how schools can influence the ways students motivate themselves by discussing the key features of optimal learning contexts that impact on students' *motivation mindsets*. It builds a motivation model that provides a window through which you can observe and reflect upon how classrooms shape student motivation and how schools impact upon teacher motivation.

The aspects of a motivating context can be categorized into four *Drivers* that impact directly on students' mindsets. These are *engagement*, which is about how the teacher tries to get to know and value the learner; *structure*, which refers to the clarity of pathways to achieving the learning goals; *stimulation*, comes from a curriculum that highlights the importance, usefulness and fun of activities and, *feedback*, which is information that allows the learner to know how he or she is progressing.

These four drivers operate along two *dimensions*. Engagement and feedback operate along the *relationship dimension*. The *power dimension* is delivered by a combination of structure and stimulation.

The relationships and power dimensions are independent dimensions, the intersection of which creates four *types of learning context*. These are the undemanding classroom, epitomized by an overprotective climate and undemanding curriculum. The *destructive* classroom is characterized by forced learning and personal blame. The *exposing* classroom is indicated by a 'prove yourself' climate and uncertainty. Key characteristics of the optimal learning context, the *motivating* classroom, include trust, autonomy, a climate of self-improvement, clarity of purpose and encouragement.

Each of the drivers and dimensions function as a continuum containing four distinct stages that are represented in the model as *gears*.

There are two main dilemmas at the heart of motivating students. The first is between trying to give students unconditional acceptance while at the same time providing them with accurate feedback. The most motivating teachers achieve this balance by moving through the relationship gears from conditional acceptance through recognition to affirmation that signals that they know and value the students.

The second major tension for teachers is to strike a balance between controlling and protecting students while releasing their potential for self-determination. This tension can be resolved by initially setting rules and imposing authority without coercion, then gradually, in a geared approach, 'letting go of the reins' to provide increasing opportunities for negotiation, choice and self-determination. In this way power assertion can be transformed into empowerment via power-sharing.

The model allows discussion about how the teacher–student relationship evolves as the class changes. At each gear the teacher plays a different role and uses a different combination of drivers. Critical events may move the class backwards into the reverse gears, including disinterest and low expectations, judgemental feedback, impossible goals and oppressive rules. An effective teacher will use each of the gears flexibly to adapt to changing circumstances. The classroom drivers are overlapping, dependent upon each other and interact in an additive and multiplicative way. High-impact teachers skillfully use each of the four drivers and their four gears switching between the gears, as the context requires, selecting the right gear of each driver for the class.

Teachers are never in neutral gear in that they never have a neutral effect. All teachers have some kind of effect on student motivation. Teachers' own motivation mindsets are 'downloaded' to students via the classroom drivers.

The four motivation mindsets are

- students' ideas about ability
- how they approach learning
- how they make sense of their progress
- how competent they feel.

Schools cannot influence student self-esteem as much as we think, but the good news is that low self-esteem is not as big a barrier to learning as we assume. Even better news is that schools and teachers can do a great deal about the mindsets that shape self-motivation. Self-esteem is more a consequence than a cause of achievement. The most important 'feel good' mindset is self-efficacy in goal achievement – the 'SEGA' factor! Self-efficacy is the belief in your own ability in particular skill areas and is different from self-esteem, which is an affective judgement of overall worth. The twin-track approach to student confidence involves, first, teaching them to think of their ability as changeable and so lead them to adopt a self-improvement attitude to achievement and, secondly, to help them make sense of progress in a way that builds their self-efficacy beliefs.

Confidence-building schools instil the belief that ability is not fixed and that there are many ways to succeed. They treat mistakes as essential steps to efficacy by linking failure to factors that students can repair. Motivating teachers encourage an accurate match between students' aspirations and their skills level. They praise student effort and strategy use and so help them focus on the process of their work and make them feel responsible for success. They help students become aware of how they are smart rather than how smart they are. They emphasize the possibility of improvement. This encourages students to put progress down to effort and concentrate on learning rather than on displaying ability. Most importantly, they stress individual rather than normative progress.

Part I

The Motivation Drivers

1 Introduction

This chapter provides a rationale for schools to move from a control culture to one that emphasizes self-motivation.

The Need for Change

Student management in Britain's schools was dominated until the 1980s by corporal punishment. Although replaced by a system of paper punishments, the predominant philosophy of corrective punishment prevailed. Phasing out of corporal punishment however stimulated for the first time in schools a need to look at the conditions that encouraged good behaviour and effective learning. In 1989 the Elton Report, a government review of discipline, moved the debate forwards by seeking a greater balance between sanctions and rewards (DES, 1989). By the late 1990s most school initiatives involved positive reward-based approaches to student management. The 1997 Education Act in England and Wales moved schools in the direction of self-discipline while retaining the traditional role of regulating behaviour and promoting a proper regard for authority. Self-discipline was also given prominence in the Scottish Education Executive's Discipline Task Group (SEED, 2001).

The trend in practice has moved from a reactive punitive approach to a reactive positive, albeit corrective approach. The control model still dominates our thinking and practice. Teachers exert most of the effort and still predominantly do things to and for students rather than with them. Students do things for or against teachers, less so with them. For self-directed behaviour to be learned, however, schools need to provide the lightest touch and the least restrictive structures necessary. The art of successful teaching is to do just enough and no more (Galvin, Miller and Nash, 1999).

There is an increasing lack of synchrony between the status given to young people by schools and by society. This book suggests that schools need to close this gap and evolve from a control culture to one involving a greater emphasis on self-motivation. Schools need to adopt the optimistic view that learning and growth is an intrinsic part of human nature that needs to be nurtured.

Young people today are experiencing an increasingly autonomous world as evidenced by their attitudes to music and fashion and their preference for watching soap operas and advertisements over children's television. Their 'mature' consumption of advertising means today's children get the toys they want, unlike previous generations who got what their parents wanted them to have.

Most parents today want their children to be assertive, self-reliant and able to make their own decisions. Nowadays, parents would not be happy if a teacher shouted at or otherwise 'overpowered' their child. Most teachers were brought up in families that were very different from their students, where parents made all the decisions. They were educated in schools where teachers dominated the classroom.

Assertiveness is a goal of anti-bullying campaigns, as well as of Personal Social Development programmes that encourage children to say 'no' to strangers and to drug-pushing peers. Schools now tell children it is not always right to do what adults tell them and that adults can be wrong.

The transformation to an increasingly autonomous youth culture is a huge challenge facing teachers, and the skills with which they resolve these tensions will be a key factor in the effectiveness of contemporary schooling. 'Youth has become adulthood without the experience, a destination reached without a journey made' (William McIlvanney).

Although the power balance between teacher and student is still asymmetrical, it is changing. Advances in communication technology challenge the idea of the teacher as the main supplier of information. The student is no longer a passive object waiting to receive knowledge from the teacher. The Internet has the potential to transform teaching into a situation where the learner is in control and where students become producers as well as consumers of knowledge.

The Transitional Reward Culture

Society is progressing towards greater affirmation and empowerment of young people. Schools are now expected to regard young people as active citizens rather than citizens-in-waiting (Learning and Teaching Scotland, 2002). The equality principle is undermining the old structures and leadership now needs to take on a new form.

While teachers are under great pressure to make more academic demands on children in the context of government drives for higher achievement, some teachers see students as increasingly challenging and harder to motivate in the new culture. They may think that worsening behaviour means we are going in the wrong direction, but the genie is out of the bottle. Teachers are unable to stop this evolution, but if they stay one step ahead they may be able to control the pace of change. Teachers who remain in the past will struggle in a conflict-and-blame swamp. Only when teachers have accepted they cannot turn the clock back will they be able to move on.

Of course, schools have not stood still and, indeed, are currently in transition. The mentality that assumed students had to be made to feel bad about themselves before they could do better has gone. Most teachers now acknowledge the need for, and benefits of, praise.

The move from a control to a reward culture however should be seen as a transition phase. Schools that have introduced rewards quickly realize they have repeatedly to refresh their approach. This constant search for new reward strategies will not lead to the holy grail (Ryan and La Guardia, 1999). At the same time the praise culture is open to criticism as a culture of indulgence (Damon, 1995).

Towards a Culture of Autonomy

This book argues that schools need to move on from the compliance culture to an emphasis on self-motivation. We need to encourage young people to invest more in themselves, to become stakeholders in and architects of their own learning. Self-discipline is what employers are looking for in young people. Lifelong learning also relies upon self-determination. Such an approach is also required to help achieve the goals of student participation recently enshrined in child care and educational legislation. Preparing students with a positive attitude to learning is probably the most important goal for schools today. Schools focus on educational qualifications but what young people will do with their qualifications will in the end be more important. For some young school leavers the problem is not a lack of job or training opportunities but their reluctance to access these because of a lack of confidence or self-determination. For others it is an inability to break away from their peer group's anti-work and anti-training culture.

This book also criticizes the conceptual wooliness of the long-held assumptions about the role of self-esteem in motivating learning, particularly that low esteem is one of the most significant roots of underachievement and high self-esteem is an asset. This has led to the belief that an important function of schools is to boost students' esteem. Trying to raise self-esteem may be of limited value as this ignores the fact that many of our feelings about our selves come from what we do rather than cause us to do it (Emler, 2001).

At the same time this book suggests that schools cannot actually affect esteem as much as we think. Esteem-building approaches are laudable but in isolation will not nurture confident learners (Dweck and Sorich, 1999). This requires attention to be focused on specific aspects of competency that are important to the student rather than vague attempts to make students feel good about themselves. The real classroom 'feel-good' factor is perhaps more accurately self-efficacy in goal achievement – the 'SEGA' factor. We motivate ourselves by thinking we can achieve our own goals by our own actions.

The Motivating School

The principles outlined in this book will also be of relevance to school managers in their attempts to lead teaching staff and create a motivating school. Child-centred teaching needs teacher-centred management, and management at all levels need to treat teachers the same way they expect teachers to treat their students. The leadership styles that have been found to create effective schools resonate with the motivating style in the classroom.

Just as parents are advised to meet their own oxygen needs before their children's in an emergency, so teachers need to nurture their own self-motivation for teaching and learning before they consider how they are going to motivate their students.

School management needs to have an overview of motivational strategies used throughout the school to maintain some consistency of student experience and to facilitate the progressive development of students' capacity to motivate themselves to learn. In this way, for example, class strategies could become increasingly sophisticated as students progress through the school in a staged way, matching the class's motivational maturation.

Aims of the Book

This book has been written to support anyone who wants to develop their understanding of motivation and skills in facilitating the motivation of young people to learn in a structured learning context. It distils and synthesizes the latest research evidence on motivation for learning and blends it with practitioners' intuitive ideas. It is not a 'quick fix' or recipe book. It provides joined-up theory, illustrated via a conceptual framework that lets teachers think about and describe their own and students' motivation. The framework generates principles that inform and endorse practice in motivating students. The principles lead to practical applications as well as core competencies.

The book tries to offer a greater understanding of student behaviour and needs, as well as providing practical advice on how to develop an optimal learning context. It provides an opportunity for practitioners to reflect on the kinds of learning environments they create and how these impact on their students' motivation. It helps elaborate our understanding of general ideas like positive attitudes. The model provides a framework that makes motivation explicit and so opens it up for a shared analysis. It provides a window through which to see what is working and not working in our schools. For school managers it allows a consideration of the kinds of environment in which teachers work.

The book aims to refine readers' intuitive ideas and help them to identify the key aspects of the self that have to be taken into consideration when trying to motivate students. To be motivating, teachers need to understand how they are motivated and how they motivate themselves.

Given the explosion of knowledge about how the brain learns, it is important to focus also on how students motivate themselves to learn. How the brain learns needs to be complemented with how the self interacts with the learning context.

Teachers have great scope to motivate and just as much scope to demotivate their students. How a teacher intuitively understands the way motivation works will shape what he or she does to motivate students. This book aims to develop readers' understanding of how their own motivation mindsets are 'downloaded' to students through the learning contexts they create. Teachers are continually making assumptions about the motives underpinning their students' performance. This book will help teachers check out the validity of these assumptions. A common assumption for example is that 'non-participation' in learning is the 'fault' of the disaffected, requiring some kind of remedial intervention. This deficit view, however, stigmatizes individuals and makes it even harder to engage them.

If students are not good at spelling, schools help them to overcome their difficulties. If students are not good at motivating themselves, schools are not sure what to do. Self-motivation is a skill that schools rely upon and expect so much of, yet teach so little. As motivation is to an extent cognitively generated, it is possible for teachers to influence students' thinking and so develop helpful motivational mindsets. Students can analyse what is going on in the classroom that helps or hinders their learning and are able to put forward sensible suggestions (Rudduck *et al.*, 1998). Making motivational processes explicit and developing a motivation vocabulary for the classroom will enable students to take charge of their own motivation. A considerable amount of material on 'teaching' motivation is currently available (for example, Mindstore, 1998; Pacific Institute, 2000; Seligman, 1998; Tuckman, 1995; Zimmerman, Bonner and Kovach, 1996).

Teachers need to accept that all students have some form of motivation and the challenge is to try to 'tune in' to what motivates students. Many students who are switched off by schools will have, for example, an encyclopedic knowledge of football league tables or the music charts. The common assumption that some students have no motivation betrays the same misunderstanding as in the assumption of the politician's wife that 'suicide bombers' have no hope, when clearly in their own terms they have a great deal of hope.

Throughout, the text deals with the motivational profile of the Western culture. The motivational profiles of other cultures may be different in significant ways but are beyond the scope of this book.

2 Current Thinking about Motivation

What is Motivation?

Motivation is an overworked and loosely used term, an umbrella term for describing all questions about why we think and behave as we do. As motivation is perhaps even more important than our ability in determining our achievement, it is important that it is understood. Motivation deals with the why of behaviour, a question that teachers often ask students. The word motivation comes from motive, which derives from the Latin *movere* meaning to move. Motivation is the sum of all that moves a person to action. To motivate means you provide a student with a motive to do something.

For the purposes of this book motivation is thought of specifically in terms of the desire to learn and the capacity to cope with challenges, setbacks and obstacles. Motivation has been seen recently as a key aspect of emotional intelligence covering the marshalling of feelings of enthusiasm, confidence and persistence (Goleman, 1996).

Motivation can be explained in terms of past learning, present activities or future goals. There is no consensus about the nature of motivation, or about the best way to analyse it. There is no one convincing theory. This book tries to develop a working model to aid our thinking about motivation which lets us better understand it and so help evaluate and develop our classroom practice.

The Functions of Motivation

Schools usually operate on a one-dimensional model of motivation, considering only the amount of motivation; students are usually considered either motivated to learn or not. It may be more helpful to think of motivation in terms of dimensions rather than categories that are either present or absent. Motivation has two main functions. First, it has a direction function, choosing among options and keeping the action as intended and, secondly, an intensity function, for example, the level of enthusiasm. The direction and intensity functions provide the evidence from which teachers can assess a student's motivation. Teachers often believe some students have no motivation. There is no such thing as an unmotivated student. Every young person has a motivational mindset, but some have more learning focused profiles than others.

Theories of Motivation

Motivational theories can be put into two camps, supported by different assumptions about human nature. Behavioural theories consider our actions to be reflexive and instinctive, governed by a 'stimulus-response' mechanism. All motivation is believed to arise from basic drives, instincts or emotions. Behavioural theories have been popular with teachers due to their apparently straightforward and easy applications. The 'carrot and stick' theory shows a deeply held assumption and popular idea that motivation is about providing rewards and punishments. According to this theory, when you motivate you are applying a stimulus, such as a reward or a threat of punishment or a combination of both.

The past 20 years have led to major changes in how motivation is defined and the constructs that are assumed to underlie it (Bandura, 1989; Covington, 1998; Eccles, Wigfield and Schiefele, 1998; Gollwitzer and Bargh, 1996; McClelland, 1985; Pintrich and Schunk, 1996; Sandstone and Harackiewicz, 2000). The most significant change has been the focus on internal processes rather than on environmental factors. Beliefs about the self play a major role in motivation from a very young age.

Current theories increasingly recognize the centrality of the self and self-determining aspects of behaviour. The greatest output of the human mind is the sense of self, the sense of who we are. Our current understanding of the self, however, is fast evolving and it is a great challenge to grasp its complexities. Individuals are no longer seen as responding to, and being manipulated by, external stimuli. They are seen as being motivated by personal goals, competency beliefs and personal evaluations of their worth. The source of motivation is seen as something inside the person. We are all highly attuned and sensitive to messages about the self throughout life. Learning and growth are seen as intrinsic parts of human nature that need to be nurtured. Motivation is generated from inside while being heavily influenced from outside. It is the interaction of the individual and his or her environment that determines motivation.

The self has a key task of self-enhancement, a basic law of human behaviour driven by our need to feel competent, autonomous and loved by others (Deci and Ryan, 1985). This is achieved by seeking out areas that offer a high chance of success; discounting the importance of and withdrawing from areas that produce failure; making sense of events to present the self in the best light; taking credit for success while being surprised at failure and treating any failure as a learning experience.

Thinking about motivation has shifted from operant learning to a cognitive approach concerned with how incoming stimulation is used. In this model students are seen as active seekers and processors of information rather than passive recipients of teacher input. Students' beliefs, thoughts, feelings and values are seen as the main influences on their behaviour.

From Theory to Practice

Education thinking has been marked for a long time by the tension between the view of education as development from within and the opposing idea that it is formation from without (Dewey, 1938). Teachers cannot make students motivated but they can set up the conditions that nurture motivated learners. It is possible to force students to perform better but a lust for learning cannot be imposed. The best teachers create a learning context that maximizes the chances of students developing interests and removes the conditions that act as constraints. The teacher's task is not to motivate students to achieve but to provide the opportunities for achievement that will be motivating. Teachers can best influence how students motivate themselves by setting up the optimal conditions that help shape their beliefs about ability, how they approach learning, how they make sense of their progress and how competent they feel.

Students' perceptions of their own ability can vary, depending on the type of task they are working on and, so, motivation will vary from setting to setting. In exploring student motivation it is important to consider the views students have of the nature of their ability, their achievement goals and their level of confidence in their ability. Motivation is consistent over time and context only so long as these variables hold constant.

Current models of motivation tend to concentrate on cognitive processes. These models assume that academic competence is the primary goal students seek at school. The social worlds of students, however, must also be included in any consideration of motivation. Social goals are strong predictors of academic achievement and the promotion of socially responsive behaviour often results in higher academic performance (Juvonen and Wentzel, 1996). The social climate of the classroom is a powerful motivator of academic as well as social behaviour.

Intrinsic and Extrinsic Motivation

We are intrinsically motivated when we want to do something for its own sake, interest and enjoyment, when we get a feeling of satisfaction during rather than after an activity (Deci, 1975). Participation is its own reward and does not depend on external reinforcements or constraints. Students are, on the one hand, intrinsically motivated to meet their needs for knowledge and understanding, a sense of competence and accomplishment, self-determination, stimulation and involvement with and approval of others (Boggiano *et al.*, 1987; Lepper and Henderlong, 2000; Sandstone and Harackiewicz, 2000). We nurture students' intrinsic motivation when we encourage their curiosity, persistence, enjoyment, mastery and independence. Extrinsic motivation, on the other hand, is a desire to act in order to make something happen that you want or to stop something that you do not want. The desire to act is stimulated by a reward outwith the individual. Equally the desire may be stimulated by avoidance of undesirable consequences. It is motivation to act as a means to an end.

Rather than thinking in terms of a dichotomy between intrinsic and extrinsic motivation, each form of motivation may also be considered as separate continua, each ranging from high to low. For any given activity, a student may have a combination of extrinsic and intrinsic motivation. For example, a young child who has very little intrinsic motivation for learning to play the piano will require a great deal of extrinsic motivation through inducements from his or her parents. As the child progresses, intrinsic motivation may increase and the need for extrinsic motivation will be correspondingly less. As these dimensions characterize students in relation to specific activities they can change over time and sudden changes in level of intrinsic motivation are not uncommon. Success in school clearly requires students to attend to both intrinsic and extrinsic sources of motivation. Working on a task for intrinsic reasons, however, is not only more enjoyable, but it also helps learning and achievement. In turn, learning helps promote intrinsic motivation.

Self-determination

Self-determination is any effort to be in control of and to alter our actions, thoughts and feelings. Its essential nature is of one action overriding another, in terms of stopping, starting or changing behaviour (Carver and Scheier, 1998). Self-determination is the degree to which we feel our actions are autonomous (Deci and Ryan, 1985; 1987; 1995). Autonomous behaviour comes from one's sense of self, unlike controlled behaviour that comes from outside pressure. Self-determination may well be the most powerful factor in becoming a well-adjusted person.

The basic features of self-determination include having a particular goal, monitoring yourself in relation to that standard and changing your response to better match the standard. Self-determination failure can happen when the student does not know the goal, when, for example, the teacher has failed to make it explicit; or when the student has conflicting standards between home and school. Self-determination problems can also occur when the student is unable to self-monitor, for example in a group of bullies where the student loses his or her sense of individuality, or when the student does not have the skills to achieve the standard because of difficulties such as listening to instructions or keeping focused.

Moving from External Regulation to Self-determination

Self-determination ranges through different types of extrinsic to intrinsic motivation (Deci and Ryan, 1985). Types of extrinsic motivation can be differentiated by the degree of autonomy in the regulation of behaviour. The different stages reflect the degree to which the value of the behaviour is internalized. This continuum is described below (see Diagram 2.1).

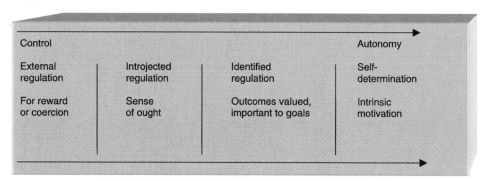

Diagram 2.1 ■ The regulation continuum

The starting point in schools is usually to get students to do what teachers tell them to do. Examples of external regulation include the teacher who uses punishment lines whenever rules are broken. Beyond compliance there is a need to encourage students to 'internalize' these rules. At the stage of introjected regulation the rules are adopted but not incorporated into the sense of self. Introjected regulation indicates that students go along with a task because they think they should and feel guilty if they do not. Such 'ought' regulation might include, for some people, studying for examinations, doing homework or visiting a sick relative or elderly parent.

With identified regulation, action begins to be integrated within the person's sense of self. For example, students who do their homework because they see it as valuable are at the identified regulation stage, while those who do it just because their parents insist remain at the introjected stage. Exercise, for example, may not in itself be enjoyable for some people but is seen as good for one's health and well-being, and so remains at the introjected stage. At the stage of identified regulation students see the benefits of the activity or rules. It is still instrumental but represents an early form of autonomy. The student makes the value his or her own, understands its rationale and experiences a sense of self-determination in acting in line with it. Although identified regulation is a self-determined form of motivation, it differs from intrinsic motivation in that it is instrumental; the behaviours it leads to are not for their own sake.

The goal of teaching should be to help students reach the stage of self-determination by gradually supporting their autonomy, giving them chances to solve their own problems and inviting them to participate in making decisions. Ultimately we want students not to be committed to our values and rules but to be able to make their own decisions about which values and rules to embrace. The best preparation for making decisions is to make decisions. Students will be more likely to internalize our values when they do not feel overcontrolled. Surveillance and conditional praise damage this process in so far as they reflect external rather than self-regulation (Deci and Ryan, 1985; 1987; 1995). Students who have been given an opportunity to participate in family decision-making and whose parents allow a degree of independence develop a higher level of interest and enjoyment in school than those not given such opportunities (Burger, 1992).

Intrinsic motivation happens spontaneously and as such cannot be coerced, but it can be facilitated. Excessive pressure can backfire by undermining exploration, curiosity, creativity and spontaneity. Children's internalized ideals from adults, for example, what their parents would ideally like them to be, can also be as pressing as external controls and can damage intrinsic motivation.

Parents trying to encourage their children into preferred activities are caught between a rock and a hard place as they realize that without directing them and giving enough exposure to the specific activity children will not become interested. But they do not want to overimpose their desires and have their efforts backfire, and undermine the intrinsic value of the activity for the children. The compromise is a difficult balancing act.

The motivation model developed here explores the key motivation mindsets that help shape self-determination as well as the practical aspects of the classroom drivers which have the most impact on these features. The model is built on cognitive theories of motivation, as they are seen to provide the most useful insights into how motivation for learning is nurtured in the classroom.

3 What Drives Motivation?

This chapter presents a model of the key classroom features or drivers and explains how they work together to influence student motivation.

We first discuss the key human motives that underpin and illustrate the centrality of the two dimensions of the motivation model.

Balancing Contradictory Motives

Being the same and different

We want to be the same as everyone else but also want to be different from others. We reconcile these conflicting goals by identifying with the common features within an 'in-group' and this oneness is reinforced by rejecting the differences of a common enemy or an 'out-group' (Brewer, 1991). This process is enacted through the Relationships Dimension. Our social identity derives from this basic tension between our need for affirmation from, and similarity with, others and our need for uniqueness. Teenage peer groups are a good example of this whereby they develop styles of appearance and behaviour that allow them to blend in with their peers while 'sticking out like a sore thumb' to their parents. Our group identity, just like our fashion style, ingeniously lets us be the same and different at the same time.

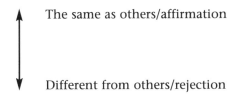

The same as others/affirmation

Different from others/rejection

We approach or avoid

Children are active, curious and playful from birth, and are naturally inclined towards learning and exploration. They have a natural inclination towards activity but also a vulnerability to passivity. Schools need to support and encourage the inclination towards constructive activity and minimize the forces that exploit student vulnerability to laziness and passivity. This is enacted through the power dimension.

Passive ◄━━━━━━━━━━━━━━► Active

At the same time we have two main competence motives, namely to seek success and to avoid failure (Atkinson, 1964). Some people generally lean more to the avoidance orientation and others more to the approach response (Higgins and Liberman, 1998). Growth-seeking individuals have a strong need to develop as people and their self-actualization needs outweigh any concerns about failure (Maslow, 1962). Consequently they see obstacles and challenges as opportunities for development (Dykman, 1998).

Avoidance ◄━━━━━━━━━━━━━━► Approach

The key interpersonal motives

Loneliness and chaos are our two greatest fears. We strive to avoid loneliness via intimacy with, and approval of, others (our relationships). We strive to avoid chaos by seeking autonomy and control over our lives (empowerment). Chaos and loneliness are often at the heart of the problems of students with motivational problems. Secure adults in contrast are characterized as being comfortable with both intimacy and autonomy (Bartholemew and Horowitz, 1991). How our two main fears drive our key motives is illustrated in Diagram 3.1.

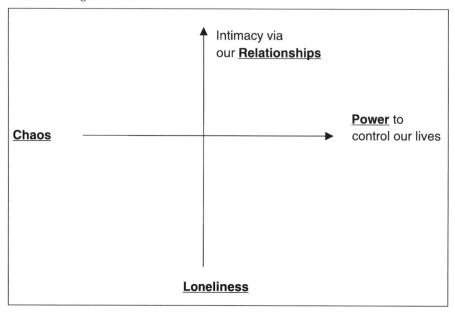

Diagram 3.1 ■ The interpersonal motives

The Drivers and Dimensions

There are four features of learning contexts that teachers employ to drive student self-motivation.

First, teachers need to communicate that they are interested in their students. They do this through the *engagement* driver that shapes the quality of the relationships between the teachers and students as well as between peers. The quality of engagement reflects the teacher's willingness to understand and get to know students. Engagement is the term often used to describe students' general involvement with learning. In this sense, however, its focus is narrowed to social and emotional engagement.

Secondly, teachers need to make it clear to students how they can achieve the desired outcomes and goals. The *structure* driver determines the amount of explicit information that is made available in the classroom. By clearly setting boundaries, communicating goals and responding consistently teachers provide the required level of structure.

Once teachers have 'set out their stall' in terms of their engagement climate and structure they can get on with the curriculum. Optimal motivation, thirdly, requires the *stimulation* driver that relates to the quality of teaching and learning in the classroom. Students are intrinsically motivated when they want to do something for its own sake, interest and enjoyment. Relevance, challenge, control, curiosity and fantasy are some of the key intrinsic motivators.

Finally, self-motivation requires the *feedback* driver that tells students how well they are doing. Motivating feedback involves praising effort and strategy use, making students feel responsible for success, stressing personal rather than normative success and linking failure to factors students can repair.

These four drivers operate along two *dimensions*. The *power dimension* is delivered by a combination of structure and stimulation. Engagement and feedback operate along the *relationship dimension*. Both dimensions are needed and, like petrol and a petrol engine, each one is useless without the other. Computerized learning could offer a form of stimulation and structure but no relationship. The teacher–student relationship is *the* vital component in the motivation to learn.

The main features of the model are presented in Diagram 3.2.

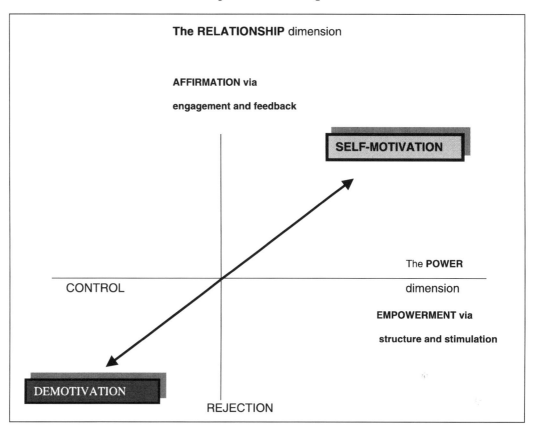

Diagram 3.2 ■ The two dimensions

How the Model Works

The model has as its cornerstone the principle that the source of motivation is internal to the self and will flourish when the classroom is sensitive to, and can meet, students' needs. Students are intrinsically motivated to meet their needs for stimulation and self-determination (that is, empowerment). Likewise they are intrinsically motivated to meet their needs for involvement with, and approval of, others and a sense of accomplishment (affirmation through relationships).

> There is clearly an overlap between the dimensions and drivers. For example, there are empowering aspects of feedback. Examples of feedback such as praise that encourages rather than controls or the allocation of responsibility rather than blame could be classified as empowering. Similarly, there can be affirming qualities of stimulation such as optimal challenge that enhances one's sense of self. Indeed, praise when it empowers becomes encouragement, and power-sharing when it affirms is experienced as trust.

The four classroom types

Diagram 3.3 shows how the two dimensions intersect to form a quadripolar model and create four classroom types. Like houseplants, students' motivation can be damaged by neglect, too much kindness or abuse.

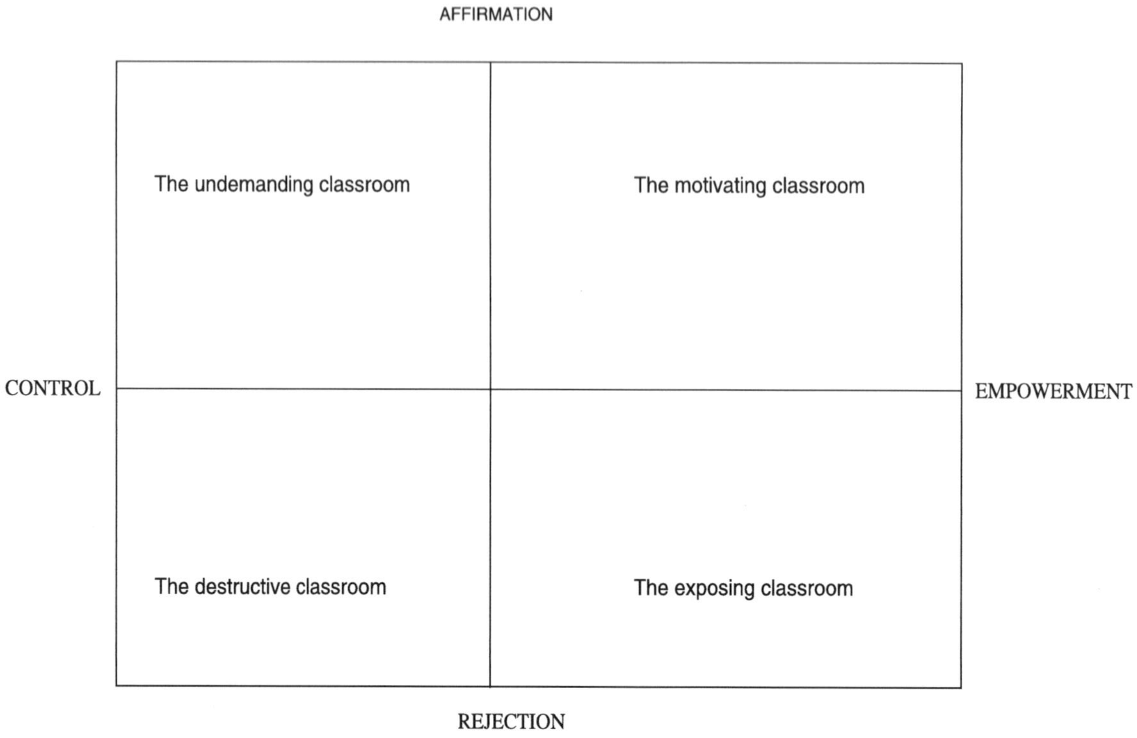

AFFIRMATION
The undemanding classroom
The motivating classroom
CONTROL
EMPOWERMENT
The destructive classroom
The exposing classroom
REJECTION

Diagram 3.3 ■ The four classroom types

Sweaty
Sunny
Chilly
Stormy

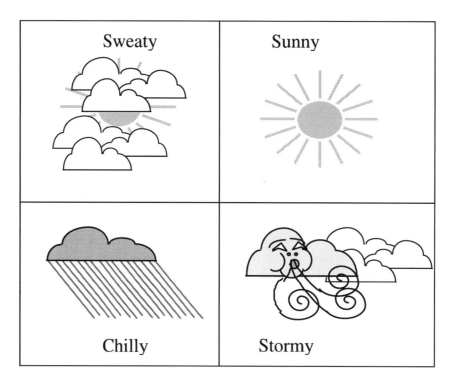

Diagram 3.4 ■ The four motivation climates

Diagram 3.4 shows the four classroom types in terms of weather conditions. Like the weather, classroom conditions can be changeable and hard to predict.

Reviews of parenting practice have also identified two major dimensions of warmth and control (Rohner, 1966). Maccoby and Martin (1983) identified four parenting styles from a combination of these dimensions that map onto the four quadrants outlined above, i.e. authoritative, authoritarian, indulgent-permissive and rejecting-neglectful. Adolescents from authoritative homes have consistently been found to show the most positive outcomes, including academic achievement (Dornbusch *et al.*, 1987; Johnson, Shulman and Collins, 1991).

The four drivers are summarized for each classroom type in Diagram 3.5.

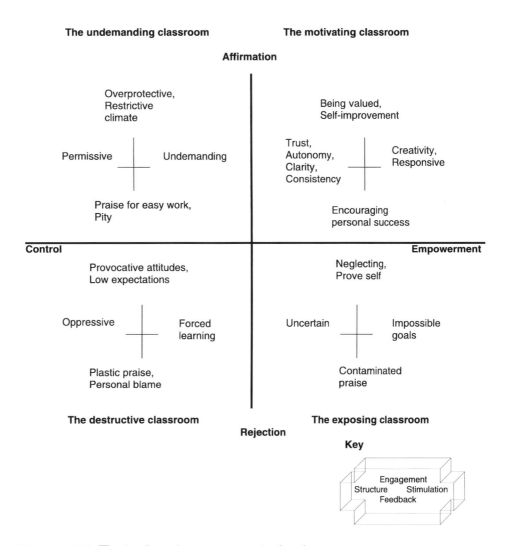

Diagram 3.5 ■ The four classroom types in detail

The *undemanding* classroom will be epitomized by, for example:
- an overprotective climate
- a restrictive climate
- a permissive structure
- an undemanding curriculum
- low expectations
- praise for easy work
- overdependency on external rewards

■ pity for failure.

The *destructive* classroom will be epitomized by, for example:

■ low expectations
■ forced learning
■ an oppressive structure
■ personal blame
■ 'plastic' praise
■ a focus on what students do wrong.

The *exposing* classroom will be epitomized by, for example:

■ a 'prove yourself' climate
■ high evaluative threat
■ uncertainty
■ a chaotic structure
■ contaminated praise, 'but why can't you do so well all the time?'
■ mean with praise
■ more interest in results than student welfare
■ some students feel overpressurised.

Key characteristics of the *motivating* classroom will include:

■ trust
■ autonomy
■ creativity, humour
■ a responsive climate
■ a sense of being valued
■ a climate of self-improvement
■ clarity of purpose and goals
■ consistency
■ an emphasis on personal success
■ encouragement and genuine praise.

The eight classroom types

The intersection of the two primary dimensions also creates two secondary axes, displayed in Diagram 3.6. The bully–nurture axis reflects the fact that bullying is at the opposite end of the continuum from nurturing self-motivation. Bullying is damaging someone else to enhance the self, while nurturing self-motivation is sacrificing the self to enhance the other person. The second continuum ranges from an overprotecting style at one end to an exposing approach at the other. In this continuum neither end is particularly desirable. The opposite end of the protect dimension is to expose to risk or danger. The optimal position in this dimension is somewhere in the middle.

The relationship dimension creates relatedness, the empowerment dimension a feeling of competency and the nurture dimension a sense of autonomy. As stated earlier, the self is driven by our need to feel competent, autonomous and related to others (Deci and Ryan, 1985; 1987; 1995).

If we consider the two secondary axes along with the two primary dimensions, we now have eight types that more accurately reflect the full range of classroom types. These are illustrated in Diagram 3.7.

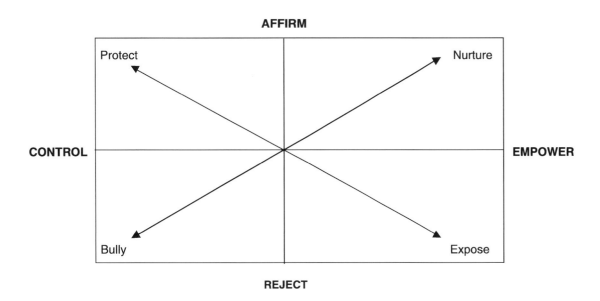

Diagram 3.6 ▨ The secondary axes

Schools are made up of a mixture of types rather than dominated by one or two.

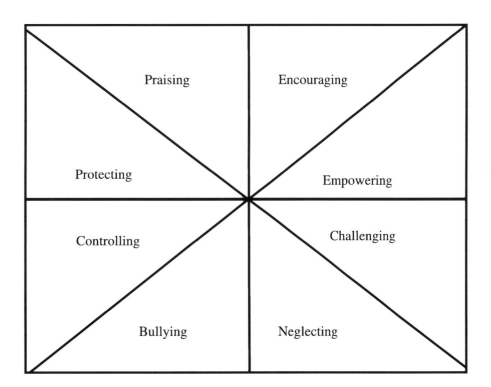

Diagram 3.7 ▨ The eight classroom types

This can be elaborated into 16 types, or zones, that further differentiate the dimensions. The pupils in any classroom can be distributed across these zones and, indeed, move dynamically throughout the zones displayed in Diagram 3.8. This vividly illustrates the level of skill and challenge involved in motivating teaching.

The relationship gears

There are two main dilemmas at the heart of motivating students. One of these tensions is between trying to give students unconditional acceptance while at the same time providing them with accurate feedback.

Students need the security of knowing their worth is valued. This does not imply, however, that teachers need to be kind to students no matter what, or that they should lower their standards. Rather, feedback should always be honest but build on strengths. Any negative feedback should be linked to specific behaviour in a way that avoids attacking the student personally. As long as students know their worth is secure they will absorb accurate feedback about what they do. The unconditional acceptance is of their worth as human beings.

Both our cultural attitudes and biology attune us to the negative. Teachers in particular are 'programmed' to be 'on the look out' for problems. They need, therefore, to consciously focus on good behaviour and move from controlling acceptance through encouragement to affirmative feedback that signals that they know the students well and value them. This is best achieved by working through the relationship 'gears', outlined below. The teacher–class relationship, just like any relationship, should be characterized, particularly in its early stages, by growth. If there is little growth the relationship is probably going backwards.

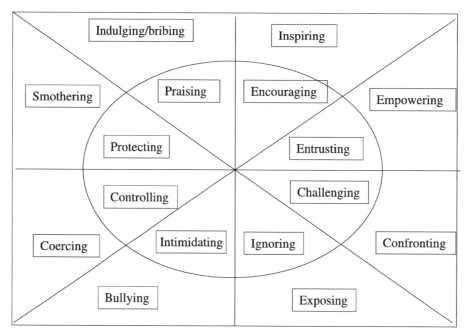

Diagram 3.8 ■ The 16 classroom types

First gear – 'conditional support'

This is the starting point for any teacher–student relationship and involves approval that is conditional upon student compliance. It includes fair punishments and criticism without attacking student self-worth. This stage gives the teacher the opportunity to get to know the students.

Second gear – 'encouragement'

This gear involves positive expectations and attitudes, recognition of achievements and accurate but empathic feedback that builds on strengths. Crucially it avoids subjective and personalized attacks on students. Students are given encouragement that makes them feel responsible for any success. This stage is critical in helping shape students' sense of identity as learners.

Third gear – 'affirmation'

In this gear the teacher communicates that the students are known well, understood and valued. Self-improvement is emphasized.

The outcome of progress through these gears will be positive self-esteem.

Reverse gear – 'rejection'

This gear includes confrontational attitudes, neglect and disinterest, or overprotection and low expectations. Empty, grudged or plastic praise (that looks like but is not the real thing) and unnecessary rewards may be given. This gear is epitomized by personalized blame that attacks students' self-esteem.

The four gears are detailed in Diagram 3.9 for both of the relationship drivers.

The RELATIONSHIP dimension Reverse gear rejection		1st gear conditional acceptance	2nd gear encouragement	3rd gear affirmation
Provocation, disinterest or overprotection, low expectations, humiliation	**Engagement**	Conditional support	Positive expectations, inclusive attitudes, recognition	Known well, valued, self-improvement
Judgemental, subjective, personalized	**Feedback**	Descriptive, objective, external rewards/ punishment	Reflective progressive-oriented information about effort and progress	Self-evaluation, pupils feel responsible for success

Diagram 3.9 ■ The relationship dimension

The power gears

The second major dilemma for teachers is to strike a balance between controlling students while releasing their potential for self-determination (Vallerand, Guay and Fortier, 1997). Control can convey interest and concern but also a lack of trust or sense of incompetence (Pomerantz and Ruble, 1998). Confidence, interestingly, is derived from the Latin *fide* meaning trust. Teachers need to protect students and give them the required security while, at the same time, encouraging responsibility. This tension can be resolved by initially setting rules and imposing authority, then gradually 'letting go of the reins' and providing increasing opportunities for negotiation, choice and self-determination. In this way power assertion can be transformed into personal power via power-sharing. The power dimension stretches from excessive power assertion to a situation where the students are empowered to take control of their own learning.

Empowerment requires, in the first instance, authoritative teachers who give a sense of direction, reasonable pressure and increasing choice within limits set in non-controlling ways. In contrast to those teachers who are driven by a fear of losing what little power they have, the more motivating teachers are those who seek co-operation and give their power away as soon as possible. This is best achieved by appropriately moving through the empowerment 'gears'.

First gear – 'power assertion'

This is the starting point for any motivating relationship with a group of students and is characterized by firm fairness and includes the basic building blocks of group management and curriculum delivery.

Second gear – 'power-sharing'

The transition to this gear is an important and challenging phase in the development of a motivating classroom and involves the building of mutual respect. At the heart of empowerment is trust, the glue that holds everything together. Accountability, as opposed to culpability, is stressed.

Third gear – 'personal power'

Once second gear is consolidated, the transition to this third gear should be relatively smooth. This has the maximum impact on the motivation mindsets by enabling a high level of self-determination.

The outcome of progress through these gears will be self-determination and intrinsic motivation.

Reverse gear – 'power failure'

Students who come into the class with an unhelpful motivational profile will push the teacher into reverse gear, epitomized by excessive or faulty power assertion, humiliation or chaos. An overstressed or 'burnt-out' teacher may also slip into certain aspects of this level, usually through fear of losing control.

The four gears are detailed in Diagram 3.10 for both of the empowerment drivers.

Impossible, unclear, irrelevant goals	Stimulation	Goal clarity, possible, appropriate, important, useful goals	Optimal challenge, performing to limits of ability, shared goals, curiosity, stimulation, fantasy, enjoyment	Control, problem-solving, decision-making, sense of competence
Destructive, forced learning		Directed learning, outcome predictable	Constructive learning, outcome negotiated	Creative learning, outcome open
Excessive or oppressive rules, chaos	Structure	Few positive, explicit, ascribed rules	Negotiated code	Pupil responsibility
Authoritarianism, poor signal clarity		Leading, authoritative, fairness, predictability	Following, mutual respect, trust	Self-control
Power failure/ overpower		Power assertion	Power-sharing	Personal power
Reverse gear		First gear	Second gear	Third gear

Diagram 3.10 ■ The power dimension

Classrooms provide support for student autonomy by giving choices that let students connect their behaviour to their own goals. Choice does not mean that students make decisions without teacher guidance or on a whim. Teachers need to build a scaffold for students that lets them make choices within increasingly flexible parameters. An effective scaffold needs constant readjustment to fit the student's growing level of maturity (Bruner, 1983). Classes may need more or less structure and teachers need to be flexible, to tighten or relax their 'grip' as appropriate in order to give the correct level of structure (Galvin, Miller and Nash, 1999).

The drivers and their gears

The four-quadrant model portrayed earlier, creating the four classroom types, needs to be reconfigured, as in Diagram 3.11, to more accurately reflect the scope of the non-optimal environments and the idea of the optimal classroom being created by the forward gears of the drivers.

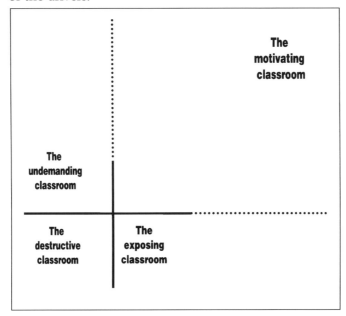

Diagram 3.11 ■ The optimal classroom

The complete driver model is presented in Diagram 3.12. The model presents the four gears of each of the four drivers. It further details reverse gear in terms of each of the three kinds of demotivating classrooms.

The reciprocal relationship between student and teacher

The model reflects the reciprocal relationship between student involvement and teacher behaviour, mediated by teacher perceptions of student motivation (Skinner, 1993). Teachers modify their behaviour towards students on the basis of their perception of student response. Teachers can be transformers or amplifiers of student motivation. Teachers are never in neutral gear and they never have a neutral effect. All teachers have some kind of effect on student motivation. They can either compensate for a student's lack of motivation or respond in such a way that magnifies the initial motivation, for example by distancing themselves from students who are disinterested in learning.

Reciprocal effects tend more often than not to magnify students' initial levels of involvement. Teachers naturally respond to motivated students with more engagement, autonomy support and positive feedback, and to hard-to-motivate students with more hostility or neglect, coercion and negative feedback. The motivationally rich get richer while typical class experiences for low motivation students alienate them further. Such motivation cycles underscore the need for senior management in schools to be aware of, and change, problematic patterns of interactions between students and teachers.

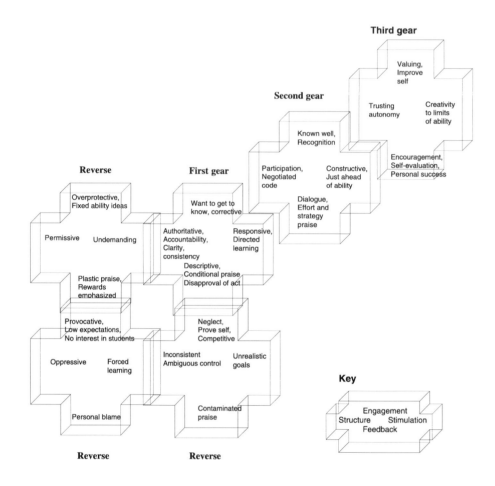

Diagram 3.12 ■ The complete drivers model

Diagrams 3.13 and 3.14 summarize the impact on students of the four quadrants.

Conclusions

Classroom and school life, of course, is not as neatly segmented as the model suggests. Clear lines do not separate one gear from another. The model, however, allows discussion about how the teacher role evolves as the class changes. At each gear the teacher plays a different role and uses a different combination of drivers. For example, as the class matures structure becomes less prominent and stimulation becomes more important. Critical events may move the class backwards into reverse gear. Sometimes it is useful to go backward to then go forward. This is illustrated by the teacher who told the unsettled class: 'Sorry you are no longer in the driving seat, I'm taking over for a while, you're in the passenger seat for the time being.' A skilled teacher will use each of the gears flexibly to adapt to changing circumstances.

It becomes problematic, however, if the teacher gets stuck in the same, usually lower, gear, when the students are mature enough to progress through the gears. The gearing can also go wrong, for example when the teacher treats students as equals without building the initial trust. Many older students become disengaged from school because they perceive

Stunted growth	Growth
Spoiled, lazy 'cotton wool kids'	'Go for it'
No growth	Distorted growth
Disaffection Cynicism	Defiance

Diagram 3.13 ■ The impact on students (1)

Cuddled	Dazzled
Muzzled	Frazzled

Diagram 3.14 ■ The impact on students (2)

a mismatch between their level of maturity and the autonomy allowed, for example, having to seek permission to go to the toilet.

In top gear, relationships continue to evolve in the form of continuous improvement. Students who are operating in the top gear will be able to self-affirm and self-empower but will continue to benefit from the drivers, particularly feedback, that will keep 'their feet on the ground'.

The classroom drivers are overlapping. They are mutually dependent upon each other and interact in a multiplicative way. A classroom without stimulation leads to boredom. A lack of structure causes chaos. Structure provides the conditions that enable optimal stimulation. Engagement allows the teacher to tune into the students' wavelength which, in turn, enables the teacher to identify what motivates the students. In particular it gives the teacher both the right and the knowledge to set realistic expectations and provide the optimal form of feedback. A classroom without engagement damages rapport, there is an inability to differentiate to meet individual needs and, at its worst, creates a sense of alienation. A lack of feedback leaves students uncertain. Ideally, all the drivers work in concert and are directed towards the same outcomes. High-impact teachers use each of the four drivers and their four gears, skilfully selecting the right gear for each of the drivers for the class.

Diagram 3.15 provides a summary matrix of the four gears of the four drivers. This grid can be used as a tool to analyse the progress of particular teacher–pupil relationships or management–teacher relationships.

	Reverse	First gear	Second gear	Third gear
Engagement	Intimidation	Correction	Empathy	Understanding
Feedback	Judgemental	Objective	Discussion	Self-evaluation
Stimulation	Destructive	Receptive	Constructive	Creative
Structure	Authoritarian	Authoritative	Trust	Autonomy

Diagram 3.15 ■ The 4 X 4 grid

As displayed in Diagram 3.16, the gears impact differentially on students' sense of self. Our self-development needs tend to grow through an ascending scale – once we have achieved one level we automatically move on to the next (Maslow, 1968). The reverse gears create a search for self-preservation in students. The essential foundations of the classroom context in first gear provide a sense of security. The features of second gear help give students a sense of identity as learners. The enhancing features of the third gear encourage a sense of self-determination.

Part III outlines the strategies that can be mapped onto this framework and practices that can be integrated into all curricular areas and classrooms as well as whole school processes. Before that, however, Part II considers the motivation mindsets that are both central in shaping self-motivation and can be directly influenced by teachers.

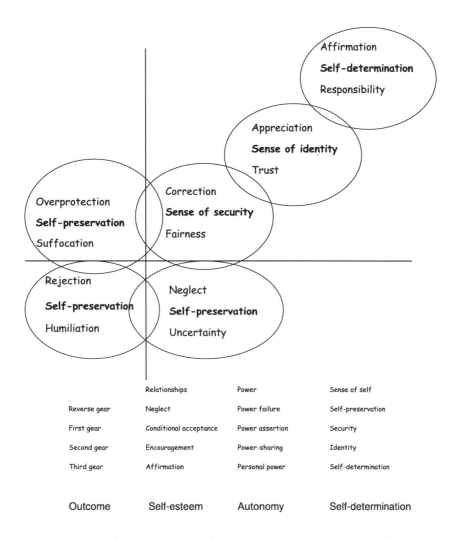

	Relationships	Power	Sense of self
Reverse gear	Neglect	Power failure	Self-preservation
First gear	Conditional acceptance	Power assertion	Security
Second gear	Encouragement	Power-sharing	Identity
Third gear	Affirmation	Personal power	Self-determination
Outcome	Self-esteem	Autonomy	Self-determination

Diagram 3.16 ■ How the gears impact on students' sense of self

The Motivation Mindsets

The motivation model proposes that the drivers of engagement and feedback deliver affirmation in the classroom, while stimulation and structure provide empowerment. The next question is, why do the drivers work? How do these drivers impact upon students' motivation, particularly their sense of self as learners?

This part outlines the four motivation mindsets that the classroom drivers can impact upon. Chapter 4 starts with students' *ideas about ability*. Then it discusses how students make sense of their successes and failures and how these *explanations of progress* influence their competency beliefs. It then goes on to describe *attitudes towards achievement* that are an integrated set of beliefs that lead to particular ways of approaching learning situations. Chapter 5 asks, what about self-esteem? It compares students with positive and negative esteem and those with contingent and high self-esteem. It considers the puzzling nature of self-esteem and where our confusion about self-esteem has led us. It then describes the key 'feel-good' factor, namely *self-efficacy in goal achievement*. The discussion looks at how the mindsets work together and the role of self-esteem in motivating learning. The final chapter in Part II looks at the important role played by learning goals.

How Teachers Make Sense of Students' Motivation

When teachers are asked to consider their students' motivation the resulting features can be categorized into four themes or components (McLean, 2003). Teachers' constructs about student motivation can be readily elicited by asking them to compare those students who are easy to motivate with those who are difficult to motivate. When teachers consider student motivation they tend to think of features that can be categorized into four themes.

Motivation starters

When teachers consider student motivation they tend to think of features that can be categorized as prerequisites of motivation for learning. Some students are hard to motivate, but the reasons are obvious and usually linked to two main factors. The first key factor is parental support and interest. If there is no support and the student's parents are either uninterested in school or are anti-school the student will be unlikely to become engaged in learning.

The second factor is the level of the student's basic self-regulation. The ideal student is an independent, focused and co-operative learner. Such students will, for example, be able to listen, pay attention and hold their concentration. They understand the purpose of school, know what they are aiming for and set tasks they can achieve. They will ask for help if needed, work well with others and have a good relationship with the teacher. Self-regulation difficulties start with reception difficulties, namely, being easily distracted and lacking concentration. Students may have organizational difficulties, be immature and overdependent. They may be used to getting their own way at home and prefer to do things on their own terms. Students with such difficulties have major barriers to self-motivation and may be thought of as at the 'pre-self-motivation' stage.

At a more advanced level, being able to carry out more sophisticated self-regulation strategies appears critical for self-motivation, particularly self-evaluation and monitoring, strategic planning and outcome monitoring (Zimmerman, 1990; 1992).

Motivation indicators

The majority of teacher constructs tend to relate to descriptions of student motivation. These tend to fall into three main categories. First, how *responsive* are the students? On the one hand, they may be focused on, and identify with, learning and show a lot of effort and persistence. Such students are enthusiastic about trying things and sustain a high level of effort. Some will be easy to get to know, keen to please the teacher and to earn praise and rewards. On the other hand, some students may fail to see the purpose of learning. These students need constant prompts. They invest all their energies in ingenious delay and avoidance strategies. They may be hard to get to know, be unresponsive to praise and have little desire or need to please the teacher.

Secondly, how *interested* are they and how much initiative do they show, for example, by searching out information for themselves? They may be disinterested in and fail to see the point of learning.

Thirdly, do they have a *positive* or negative attitude? The former will be responsive to challenge, the latter will be unable to cope with challenge or setbacks.

Outcomes

Teachers commonly regard self-esteem as a vital ingredient of motivation. This assumption is re-evaluated in Chapter 5. In the motivation model self-esteem is considered a consequence of motivation and represented as the *outcome*.

The motivation mindsets

There is a set of factors that are often missing. Apart from references to self-belief, the mindsets are rarely articulated in teachers' reflections about student motivation. This is probably because they are beyond their intuitive knowledge. The missing component is the *mindsets*, the facets of the self that power self-motivation and are influenced by the drivers.

The four components are illustrated in Diagram II.1.

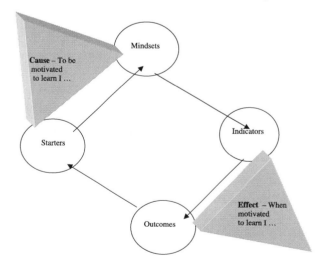

Diagram II.1 ▣ The motivation components

Part II builds on these intuitive descriptors and searches for a deeper understanding of the 'beyond-intuition' mindsets that lie behind student motivation. Part III discusses how the school and classroom drivers can impact on these mindsets.

4 Ideas about Ability, Explanations of Progress and Attitudes towards Achievement

Ideas about Ability

Students build up beliefs and assumptions about the self in order to make sense of their lives. These theories or generalizations about the self create a meaning framework for students. They lead them to interpret events in ways that can make some students vulnerable and others robust in the face of setbacks and challenges (Dweck, 2000; Hong et al, 1999).

From an early age, students are encouraged to evaluate their own and others' ability, and in this way they build up their ideas about ability. It might not appear obvious but students tend to think about ability in one of two ways. Some students see intelligence as a fixed trait, as something they only have so much of and about which there is nothing they can do. They hold what has been termed an '*entity*' theory. Students with entity beliefs think of ability in the same way as we think of the speed of a car being limited by its engine capacity. Those who in contrast have an '*incremental*' view think it can be increased through effort. The '*incremental*' view helps students realize there are many factors underlying their progress.

These relations also apply in the physical and social world (Erdley and Dweck, 1993). Those who hold an entity theory of personality are more concerned about judgements in social situations than those who hold an incremental view. This leads to greater vulnerability to pessimistic interpretations of social difficulties and, so, a lack of persistence in their social interactions. Intelligence is not the key issue for very young children. They are more concerned about ideas of goodness and badness, and see their mistakes and failures in that light (Dweck, 2000). They are trying to work out what makes someone a good or a bad child. Even pre-school children have well-developed ideas about their goodness and badness (Stipek, 1995).

Both *entity* and *incremental* students may realize the importance of ability but define it differently. Entity students may see any task as measuring their overall intelligence and, perhaps, even their overall self-worth, while incremental theorists may see the same tasks as only measuring their current ability at the particular task, that is, their self-efficacy or competency.

Explanations of Progress

The power of attributions

An attribution is the inference we make about the causes of behaviour. Individuals' beliefs about the causes of success and failure are the basic building blocks of achievement-related behaviour (de Charms 1968; Weiner 1974; 1986; 1992). Our reasoning about success strongly influences our self-efficacy beliefs. Self-efficacy is an individual's evaluation of his or her capabilities on a particular task (Bandura, 1989). The accuracy of an attribution is not important for it to have any impact. Making sense of the world comes down to subjective perceptions, as happens in the stock market where stability is determined by the perceived confidence factor rather than any objective reality.

We are more likely to perform an 'attributional search' and think about the reasons for outcomes when a learning situation is relatively new, unexpected, of great interest or importance, or when the outcome is negative. We are also more likely to create a mental 'action replay' and contemplate the causes of failure than of success. Our attributions provide a window into our biases and predict our future behaviour, frame our problems and help shape our goals (Dweck and Sorich, 1999).

The power of attributions comes from how they are categorized along four dimensions, namely, locus, stability, breadth and control.

Locus

The locus dimension concerns whether a cause is perceived as internal or external to the person. For example, ability and effort are internal whereas task difficulty and luck are external. Some students believe their lack of progress is their fault ('I'm no good at maths' – internal), while others put it down to the teacher or to other circumstances ('she can't teach' – external). If individuals experience a success and attribute it to an internal cause, they are likely to experience an increase in self-efficacy. Any failure attributed to internal causes may result in a lowering of competency beliefs in relation to that skill.

Stability

The stability dimension refers to whether the cause is stable or unstable across situations and over time. Some students will attribute failure to an enduring cause ('I'll never be any good at art') while others will see the cause as short term ('that was a hard test').

Breadth

The breadth of attributions can range from global to specific. Some students believe that the cause of any failure undermines everything else they do ('I'm just no good at school' – global), while others limit the cause to a narrow area ('I just can't do maths' – specific).

Control

This dimension involves how much control a student has over a cause and is closely linked to feelings. One feels guilty when the causes of personal failure are due to controllable factors. Shame, in contrast, is more likely to be experienced when personal failures are due to uncontrollable factors such as low competence. Guilt due to, for example, lack of effort can be motivating, while shame due to, for example, perceived low aptitude may discourage students.

Even though there are an infinite number of attributions, they can all be categorized along these dimensions and placed in the matrix in Diagram 4.1.

Perception of control is an outcome of the three other dimensions. Internal and stable attributions are typically controllable, while external and unstable explanations suggest lack of control. Global attributions indicate less control. Feeling in control is a key factor in building self-efficacy (Skinner, Wellborn and Connell, 1990).

Pessimists tend to explain failure in terms of internal, stable and global causes, and positive events in terms of external, unstable and specific causes. Conversely, optimists see negative events as due to external, unstable, and specific causes and positive events as due to internal, stable and global attributes. This attribute set gives them the sense that success is within their control.

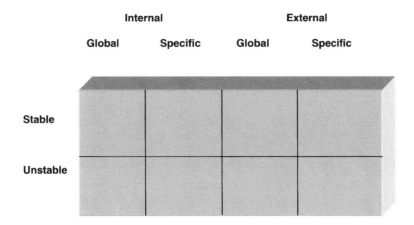

Diagram 4.1 ■ The key attribution dimensions

How attributions are shaped

Explanations for negative events are almost automatic but exist on the edge of awareness. Students' causal attributions stabilise into a style by about age nine (Nolen-Hoeksema, Girgus and Seligman, 1986) and students can get themselves into explanatory ruts (Shatte *et al.*, 1999). It would be helpful, therefore, to teach students to identify their attributions, help them see their consequences and encourage them to think of alternative ways of explaining their progress (Craske, 1988).

There are an infinite number of reasons used to explain why we succeed or fail. Success and failure are often attributed to prior achievement, some ability factor, an effort factor, the difficulty of the task, luck, help or hindrance from others, mood and health, interest and fatigue. The two most frequent attributions are ability and effort (Weiner, 1974). Teachers and students are constantly asking themselves: 'Did the student fail because he or she did not try hard enough or because he or she is not able?'

Both situational and personal factors influence the perceived causes of success or failure. Situational factors include information about the task, in particular task difficulty as well as social norms and teacher feedback. Personal factors include prior beliefs about the work and students' ideas about themselves, especially their ideas about their ability and expectancy for success.

Students' ideas about ability

Students' ideas about ability can lead them to interpret events in ways that can make some vulnerable and others robust in the face of setbacks and challenges. In understanding progress, *entity* students may focus on their fixed ability and so explain failure in terms of lack of ability rather than lack of effort. In contrast, *incremental* students, who think ability can be increased through effort may be more mastery orientated and are more likely to make effort attributions. When faced with failure they will look for ways to improve through more effort or remedial action.

Expectancy for success

How students respond will depend on their expectations of achieving the outcome and the value placed on the outcome (Wigfield, 1984). Expectancy refers to estimates of probable success but not necessarily that the students themselves are the cause of their success. Thus it is different from self-efficacy that reflects the extent to which individuals believe themselves able to succeed. These elements – expectancy, students' perceptions of competence and value – determine the motivation level. The strength of motivation to a particular action thus depends on both the value of the outcome and the expectancy of achieving it. Only when both are positive can motivation be said to exist. The two dimensions are displayed in Diagram 4.2.

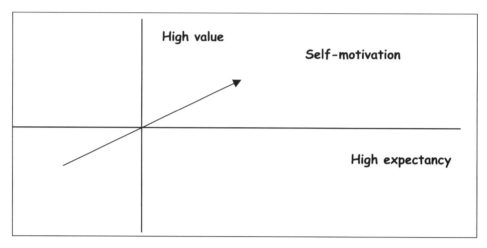

Diagram 4.2 ■ A two-dimensional model of motivation

Attitudes towards Achievement

Introduction

This section describes attitudes towards achievement that form a set of beliefs that lead to particular ways of approaching and responding to learning situations. It outlines the two main success-seeking attitudes towards achievement, as well as the two failure-avoiding styles.

Besides specific goals, students have attitudes towards achievement which are personality-like styles that generalize across different situations. These attitudes influence how students approach and respond to a learning situation (Duda, 1992; Dweck, 1988). Just as students coming into new classrooms have a tendency to sit in a particular place, the back, front or middle row, so students approach learning situations in different ways. Some may see them as tests of their ability while others see them as opportunities for learning. The attitudes towards achievement are cognitive expressions of the two main competence motives, namely, the need to achieve and the need to avoid failure.

The need to achieve – the mastery and performance attitudes

Achievement behaviour is directed at either developing or demonstrating ability. Some students adopt a mastery (or learning or self-improvement) attitude to achievement. Often referred to by their teachers as 'go for it kids', their main goal will be to learn and increase their skills. Mastery students define success in relation to their own progress. They tend to be confident and optimistic, and seek feedback for what they have done so that they can continue to improve. Effort is seen as leading to success. They cope well with failure that they see as a necessary part of learning.

A performance (sometimes called competitive or self-promotion) mindset, in contrast, represents a focus on relative ability and how ability will be judged. The main goal is to perform well to show capability of a particular skill. Students with this mindset are concerned about their ability and try to show they are smarter than others. They usually define success in relation to the progress of others. For performance students, ability means doing better than others or being successful with little effort. Mistakes suggest low ability.

Mastery students are motivated to achieve *their* best while performance students are motivated to be *the* best. An example of the performance mindset includes the person who, when told about what some people are doing, always need to go one better to 'out do' everyone else. The performance goal is to *look smart* while the Mastery goal is to *get smarter*. The performance goal is concerned with measuring ability, while the mastery goal is to master new skills.

Mastery is in most ways preferable, characterized by a concern to achieve mastery over the subject rather than with showing oneself to be better than others. Generally it leads to optimistic attributions, positive feelings, high levels of engagement, more effort and persistence. Central to a mastery mindset is a belief that outcome depends on effort, and it is this belief that leads to greater persistence. In contrast, a performance mindset can lead to pessimistic attributions, less engagement, withdrawal of effort and failure to persist.

The performance goal is a validation-seeking goal that appeals to those students who feel they need continually to prove their worth, while the mastery goal is growth-seeking. Validation-seeking students tend to feel 'up' when succeeding but 'down' when they fail (Baldwin and Sinclair, 1996).

The mastery and performance mindset are not opposite ends of a continuum or mutually exclusive of each other. Both are independent dimensions that represent different types of strivings towards achievement. It is therefore possible to be high or low in both, or to have various high–low combinations. Both goals are natural and necessary, and so a mixture of both might enhance motivation (Barron and Harackiewicz, 2000).

Striving to outperform others is not inconsistent with trying to attain task mastery. Students who adopt both goals may be at an advantage in that each goal may offset the downside of the other. Mastery goals promote task involvement and keep performance students focused on their work. Performance goals could help mastery students stay focused on what needs to be done and stop them from getting lost in their work.

Successful sports men and women need to hold a performance mindset when in competition but cannot afford to see failure as reflecting their skills or potential. In training they will be mastery orientated and will learn from their mistakes, work hard and seek ways to improve.

There are two problems, however, with a performance attitude. First, proving one's ability can take too much prominence and force out learning goals. Secondly, while a performance attitude is helpful when accompanied by a mastery attitude, it becomes problematic when it is coupled with low perceived competence.

Overstriving

Overstriving reflects an intense desire both to succeed and to avoid failure. Overstriving students worry that they are not really as smart (and worthy) as their outstanding record would suggest. Perfection is not the same as the healthy pursuit of excellence. It is being driven and constantly unhappy with yourself and your achievements. Overstrivers are often too effective for their own good because, eventually, their successes become an intolerable burden (Covington and Omelich, 1987). Raising one's aspirations after success is a natural reaction. But for the perfectionist, setting one's sights higher and higher becomes an obsessive ritual. Overstrivers cannot moderate their self-demands since perfection is their goal. As a result they experience no grace in failure, nor can they exercise self-forgiveness. The number of professional sports men and women taking performance-enhancing drugs exemplifies the power of an overstriving attitude.

Consequences for coping with failure

A performance attitude leads to a tendency to see low ability as the main cause of any failure. Such students tend to think that the harder they try, the less ability they have, which can lead them to avoid effort to protect their self-worth. Those students who have both a performance attitude and a belief in fixed ability tend to see failure as measuring their ability and are consequently vulnerable to a fear of failure. Difficulties are seen as leading to failure, which in turn provokes a negative reaction and, so, they will give up easily. They are self-critical and may come to believe in the inevitability of failure. Belief in their ability is precarious and they are consequently pessimistic and preoccupied with their self-image (Roeser, Midgley and Urdan, 1996). They may feel they have to win at all costs and so may be more likely to cheat.

Mastery students are more likely to see a link between effort and progress and make more effort attributions for failure. For them success leads to pride and satisfaction and failure leads to guilt, feelings generated by attributions that stress the controlability of behaviour. Those who believe that ability can be developed are more likely to maintain a mastery response to failure. Mastery students see difficulties as a challenge and they cope well with obstacles, and so are not easily put off.

Fear of failure

It is wrong to assume that disengaged students are unmotivated. On the contrary, some may be highly motivated, but to avoid failure rather than to succeed (Elliot and Church, 1977). Some students work hard for success without worrying about failure. Others, however, think less about succeeding than about avoiding failure.

One of the main driving forces behind achievement is emotional anticipation. On the one hand, success-seeking students anticipate pride in their accomplishments, a feeling that pushes them towards further successes. On the other hand, students with a fear of failure tend to dread further shame. Fear is probably the biggest inhibitor of motivation.

The self-concept includes ideas about who we are at present but also about our future possible selves (Markus and Ruvolo, 1989). These include the 'ideal' self and the 'ought' self (both approach goals) and the feared self (avoidance goals). Some people lean more to the avoidance orientation and others more to the approach response, and these tendencies can lead to differences in well-being (Elliot and Harackiewicz, 1996; Higgins and Silberman, 1998).

A discrepancy between the actual and the ideal self triggers an approach orientation, a moving towards the ideal goal to reduce the mismatch (Higgins, 1987). When such a goal is achieved the person will feel elated; when the goal is not achieved the feeling will be one of dejection (Higgins, 1989). The approach orientation is challenging but clear, as you just need to find the right path to your goal and take it. This can be encouraged in students, for example by suggesting they create a metaphor of themselves as a powerful person, by asking them to choose one of their heroes as a role model and suggesting that, before doing anything, they think what their hero would do.

Any mismatch between our actual and ought self evokes a moving from the proscribed to the prescribed value (Higgins, 1987). The 'ought' self reflects a sense of duty, a self you feel compelled to be rather than perhaps want to be. The main motives are to prevent the disapproval of others and to move away from the unwanted self. When such a goal is achieved the person will feel relieved, when the goal is not achieved the feeling will be one of agitation (Higgins, 1989). Agitation is a feeling that drives the behaviour of some teachers. Students (and teachers) dominated by avoidance goals have to prevent all the potential pitfalls that might happen to them and, consequently, they lead difficult lives (Pintrich and Schunk, 1996).

These dynamics are illustrated in Diagram 4.3.

Students whose fear of failure is stronger than their motivation to achieve prefer easy or very difficult tasks. They are certain of succeeding at an easy task and can rationalize failing a difficult task. Teachers can pre-empt such pupils choosing overly difficult tasks by giving them restricted choices.

Students with relatively high motivation to achieve are likely to want to move on to more difficult tasks following success and to backtrack to easier tasks following failure. Students with the alternative style, however, may move to more difficult tasks following failure at tasks that were judged initially to be easy.

Students feel the most shame with a mixture of high effort and failure and least shame with low effort and failure. This helps to explain why failure-avoiding students often do not try. Trying and still failing poses a serious threat to their self-worth. Teachers, however, tend to reward students who try and punish those who do not. Effort can become a 'double-edged sword' for many students who must balance the need for effort to please the teacher and no effort at all to protect their self-worth (Covington and Omelich, 1979).

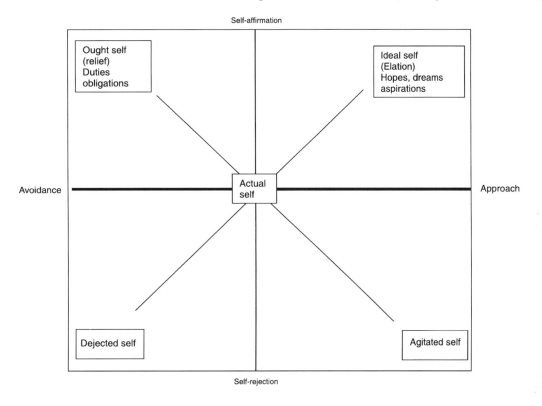

Diagram 4.3 ■ Our different selves

Trying is risky for some students because working hard and still failing suggests low ability (Kun, 1977). By not working, the causes of failure become obscured. Pressing such students to try harder in the face of failure often causes further resistance. Teachers can try to encourage achievement by rewarding hard workers and punishing the indifferent. Yet what is most important to some students is not receiving rewards from their teachers for trying hard, but finding ways to avoid the implications of too much effort while risking failure. This is a major trigger for some students to reject learning goals and hide in the camouflage of disruptive behaviour, bullying or truancy.

Helplessness

Students with an acute fear of failure may develop a helpless response when they learn over time that they have no control over events (Diene and Dweck, 1980; Peterson, Maier and Seligman, 1993). They see no relation between their effort and the attainment of their goals, and come to believe they are good at nothing. Such learned helplessness reflects a loss of hope which accompanies a belief that no matter how hard one tries, failure is inevitable (Coyne and Lazarus, 1980). This sense of helplessness is a key feature of depression and is marked by a perceived lack of control over one's world and future (Abramson, Metalsky and Alloy, 1989).

Learned helplessness comes from a tendency to put down lack of success to lack of ability that is seen as being beyond personal control. If work becomes difficult, they will give up rather than try harder. Attempts by teachers to offer help are likely merely to be seen as confirming their lack of competence. Once established, the helpless pattern is difficult to break, as such students have a tendency also to overly assimilate events and feedback into their view of themselves as hopeless.

Optimists respond positively to setbacks by making a plan or by looking for help, while students with learned helplessness assume there is nothing they can do and so do nothing, assuming the problem is due to a permanent personal deficit (Seligman et al., 1995).

Self-protection

When poor performance is likely to reflect low ability, a situation of high threat is created. Some students do better when the threat is lifted by a mitigating circumstance that allows failure to be put down to something other than one's ability (Thompson, 1999). Self-worth protection dominates some students when they anticipate poor performance that will be put down to their ability and there will be no excuses to let them 'off the hook' (Covington, 1992). Such anticipated attributions trigger efforts to keep control of the situation in contrast to the retrospective attributions of past performance that lead to learned helplessness. Self-protection is probably more common among students with inflated or volatile self-esteem (Chapter 5).

Students can have quite different ideas about the qualities that are being evaluated in achievement situations (Molden and Dweck, 2000). For some students, these have deeper meanings about the self than for others. Some people think that tasks (such as speaking or playing an instrument in public) measure fundamental, global and permanent ability, while others think they merely measure their current level of a specific acquirable skill. Such concerns come from the belief that achievement tasks measure one's fixed and global ability and that performance has implications for one's self-worth. If someone thinks that a performance task simply indicates their current level of progress on an acquirable skill, they will not put themselves under so much pressure.

Self-worth protection helps explain a number of different strategies, most commonly withdrawing effort to avoid the negative effects of poor performance. It may lie behind much of oppositional behaviour from students who challenge any form of reprimand or students who find it hard to accept praise. Another example is 'self-handicapping' (Higgins, Snyder and Berglas, 1990; Zuckerman, Kieffery and Knee, 1998), illustrated by, for example, students who get drunk the night before an examination or young people who play football with their hands in their pockets. The handicap is used to blur the link between poor performance and ability, making it hard for anyone to infer low ability. In this sense staffroom cynicism may at times be a similar smokescreen designed to protect cynics from their own limitations.

Procrastination is another form of self-worth protection and is linked with perfectionism (Burka and Yuen, 1983; Ferrari, Johnson and McCown, 1995). Frequent tests have been found to work better than regular homework in improving achievement for such procrastinating students, because they create the necessary regular incentives to learn (Tuckman, 1995). Defensive pessimism, where students hold extremely low expectations and worry about their worst nightmares coming true is another form of self-worth protection.

Self-worth protection is probably more likely among boys and learned helplessness more common with girls (Ruble et al., 1993). It may be common among boys who present a 'couldn't care less front'. Such students can believe that they could be successful if they could be bothered. Girls may be more likely to make pessimistic attributions and see failure as evidence of low ability and give up trying. As showing ability is often more important for boys, they will make more excuses when their ability is called into question.

The four attitudes to achievement are portrayed in Diagram 4.4, where they are framed in relation to the dimensions of fear of failure versus success-seeking and self-affirmation versus comparing self to others.

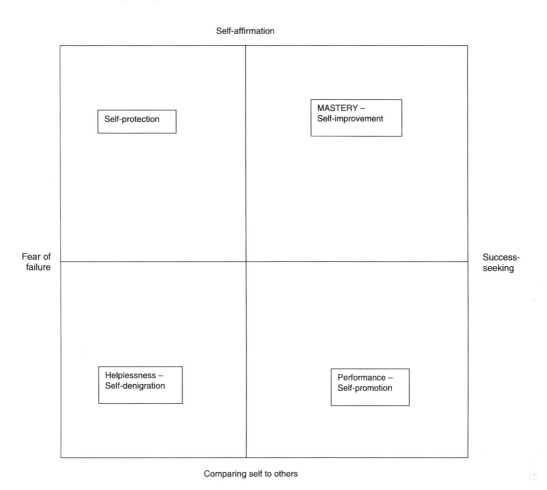

Diagram 4.4 ■ Attitudes towards achievement (1)

The four achievement attitudes are compared in detail in Diagram 4.5. This grid provides an analytical tool to compare and contrast students' response to various strategies such as praise, rewards, punishments and forms of evaluation.

Mastery You want to get smarter	Performance look smarter	Self-protection avoid looking stupid	Helplessness you have given up
You try to do your best	be the best	make out you do not care	avoid further humiliation
You believe ability is changeable	fixed	fixed	fixed
You are confident in your ability	unsure	keen to protect your ability	sure you are the least able
You can get smarter by working hard	effort counts up to a point	effort does not count	failure is inevitable
Learning is a chance to improve	a test of your ability	a threat	beyond you
You measure progress on your terms	being better than others	being better than others	avoiding failure
You feel confident and in control	You are anxious if you think you are not up to it	You think you would be successful if you tried	Life just happens to you
You see failure as a part of learning	to be avoided at all costs	down to bad luck	inevitable
You are resilient	You are only as good as your last success	You give up if you think you might fail	You opt out
You pursue excellence	You may be a perfectionist	You procrastinate and make excuses	You do not engage
You set personal goals	competitive goals	easy goals	You do not have goals
Grades are means to an end	what it is all about	what it is all about	beyond reach
You will be hard when self-assessing	You will cheat	You will cheat	You will refuse
You prefer work you learn a lot from	You can be successful	at easy tasks	difficult tasks that help you rationalize failure
You ask for help when you need to	You see help as a chance to do better	You see help as a chance to be given the answer	as confirming the worst
You see criticism as a way to improve	as a challenge	never accurate	You expect it
You enjoy praise	You love public praise	You want praise	You find it hard to accept, worry you have to live up to it

Diagram 4.5 ■ Attitudes towards achievement (2)

Where attitudes towards achievement come from

There are many factors shaping students' attitudes towards achievement, including their parents' beliefs (Ames and Archer, 1987) and their classroom experiences (Ames, 1992; Ames and Archer, 1988). Of particular significance are students' ideas about ability and their explanations for success and failure.

Ideas about ability

Entity ideas about ability tend to lead to performance goals. When ability is seen as fixed, students become concerned with showing what ability they have. They tend to focus on their performance rather than learning to gain positive judgements of their intelligence. In understanding progress, entity students may also focus on their fixed ability and explain failure in terms of lack of ability more than effort, making them vulnerable to failure. Such a focus on performance goals leads to a lack of persistence in the face of setbacks. In both learning and social situations, students who blame their abilities for failure or rejection tend to give up to avoid further setbacks. In contrast, when students hold an incremental notion, they tend to focus on learning.

Students who enter the classroom with a fixed intelligence view look out for positive judgements of their intelligence. This goal makes them especially sensitive to cues signalling failure, leading them to perceive any setbacks as failure and to attribute these problems to their lack of ability. This in turn sets in motion not only a cycle of negative feelings and poor performance, but also a tendency to adopt defensive strategies such as escaping from the situation or minimizing effort. In contrast, students who hold an incremental view of ability are more likely to focus on the task, display greater involvement and be less preoccupied with seeing learning as a test of their worth.

Explanations for success and failure

Success-orientated and failure-avoiding students hold different explanations for their successes and failures. The attribution pattern associated with success-seekers is positive and uplifting. They tend to believe they can handle most academic challenges and attribute success to a mixture of ability and effort, and failure to lack of effort. Success gives confidence in one's ability, whereas failure signals the need to try harder. They are not threatened by failure because it does not reflect on their ability. Thus failure can be used to motivate already successful students.

Failure-avoiding students tend to attribute their lack of success to a lack of ability and put down success to external factors such as luck or an easy task. They blame themselves for failure but take little or no credit for success. They are demoralized by failure because they feel unable to correct the situation. Any success only implies an obligation to do well the next time. They may even sabotage their efforts when they find themselves in danger of succeeding. Students' motivation to avoid failure is shaped partly by the level of anxiety they experience as a result of failure. Girls generally are more likely to express negative, failure-prone attributions than boys (Ruble et al., 1993).

Parenting

Several aspects of parenting appear particularly influential upon students' achievement attitudes (Ames and Archer, 1987; Goodnow and Collins, 1990; Gottfried, 1994; Jacobs and Eccles, 2000). Even as early as 1 year old, secure attachments and supported autonomy leads to children with a mastery attitude.

Parents show distinct differences in how they view learning, and their views are shaped by the achievement goals they hold for their children. They vary in the priority they give to their child being successful versus being a hard-worker. Most parents want their children to be successful and hard-working. Some parents, however, place greater emphasis than others on normative standards. Such parents are only interested in norm-based feedback about their children's progress. Parents with performance attitudes to achievement rate the value of schoolwork in terms of the probability of success and prefer to avoid challenging tasks for their children.

The extent of the value placed on effort is dependent on parents' achievement attitudes. Performance-orientated parents put more emphasis on ability. Mastery parents are more concerned about their children's efforts and active participation. They prefer high effort from their children and are more likely to attribute their children's success to effort.

Mastery-orientated parents expect their youngsters to achieve success. From an early age they encourage their children to try new things, to explore options and to exercise independence. These parents also provide a great deal of nurturing so that their children will acquire the skills necessary for independence (Baumrind, 1991). They tend to reward praiseworthy accomplishments and ignore disappointing performances.

Failure-avoiding parents tend to react badly to failure, see it as unacceptable and punish accordingly, while success is met with faint praise or indifference. Another destructive parental reaction is inconsistency – a tendency to punish failure sometimes and ignore it at other times or, even, reward poor performances (Kohlmann, Schumacher and Streit, 1988). Such unpredictability is implicated in the development of learned helplessness.

A further unhelpful parenting style involves overbearing demands for excellence but with limited support to achieve it (Davids and Hainsworth, 1967). Parents who do not hesitate to enrol a very young and immature child in school rather than consider delaying his or her entry illustrate this attitude. With overbearing parents the child hopelessly maintains unrealistically high goals but has no way to attain them. These parents demand excellence and nurture the intellectual tools but pressure the child by punishing failure. In this way they create self-protective or overstriving attitudes in their children. Procrastination has been linked to such unrealistic parental expectations and imposed standards of perfectionism.

5 The Real 'Feel-Good' Factor – Self-efficacy in Goal Achievement

This chapter asks, what about self-esteem? It compares students with positive and negative esteem and considers contingent and high self-esteem. It reflects upon the puzzling nature of self-esteem and where our confusion about it has led us. It moves on to a description of the most important 'feel-good' factor, namely, self-efficacy in goal achievement. The discussion looks at how the motivation mindsets work together and, finally, reviews the role of self-esteem and its connections with the mindsets in motivating learning.

What about Self-esteem?

Self-esteem has been paid more attention than probably any other psychological idea and is one of the few commonplace psychological terms in public use. But what is it and what is its role in motivating learning?

Self-esteem is our overall view of the degree to which we see ourselves to be an 'OK' person, dependent on the criteria we use to determine 'OK'. It is not just the sum of our judgements about the self; it shapes those judgements and affects the ways in which evidence about the self is interpreted.

Self-esteem has been considered to be an attitude toward the self (Rosenberg, 1965). Like all attitudes, it has both cognitive and affective components. It is often thought, however, that self-esteem is fundamentally based on the feelings we have about ourselves (Brown, 1993).

Although it is often confused with self-efficacy, it is different from perceptions of efficacy, which are judgements about abilities in specific areas. Self-esteem is more an affective and diffuse judgement of our worth than an appraisal of ability to develop a specific skill. Another way of seeing the distinction, perhaps, is that self-efficacy is an important aspect of self-esteem, the skill-specific form of self-esteem.

Self-esteem is set in two main ways. First, it is set by the ratio of our successes to aspirations (James, 1950). If you see yourself as competent in areas where you are keen to do well, for example in your career or more specifically in a particular sport, you are more likely to have high self-esteem. Conversely, if you fall short of your ideals in areas where you want to be competent, you may have low self-esteem. A lack of competence in areas that are unimportant to the self may not adversely affect self-esteem.

Secondly, self-esteem is partly a social creation that is largely a product of our interaction with others. Our assessment of our own worth is based on the judgements we think others make of us (Cooley, 1902). The self is constructed by looking into the social mirror to find out the opinions of significant others towards the self. If they hold the self in high regard, self-esteem should be high.

How self-esteem develops

Very young children's sense of self-esteem is, not surprisingly, based upon concrete descriptive characteristics (Stipek, Rechia and McLintic, 1992). Young children between 4 and 7 years old tend to inflate their sense of adequacy because they are unable accurately to use social comparisons to self-evaluate and their parents usually give consistently positive feedback. In middle childhood, the somewhat fantasy-based confusion of actual with ideal self is replaced with the use of social comparison. Negative as well as positive self-evaluations are now present in what is a more accurate self-assessment. By then students have adopted our cultural preoccupation with how we are different from one another and with who is the 'best'. Most students can accurately rank the competence level of every member of their class.

Somewhere around the age of 7 or 8, students start comparing themselves to their peers in a way they have not done before. They have formed an internal model, not just of the significant others in their lives, but also of themselves. They learn about themselves by comparing themselves to others with whom they share a social category, the others in the group of people 'like me'.

Around this age students develop domain-specific evaluations of their competence in addition to a more global concept of their worth. The most important domains have been found to be scholastic competence, athletic competence, social acceptance, physical appearance and behaviour (Harter, 1983). Students judge scholastic competence and behaviour to be most important to parents and social acceptance, physical appearance and athletic competence to be most important to peers. Throughout life physical appearance and then social acceptance have been found to be the most important contributors to self-esteem. Competencies in scholastic and sport domains take third place.

Three further areas are included in adolescent descriptions of self, namely, close friendships, romantic appeal and job competence (Harter, 1983). The main task of adolescence is to form a coherent and consistent identity that will provide a platform for adult life. In adolescence a tendency to feel the evaluation of significant others and the social world at large leads to self-criticism and to instability of self-esteem. The critical identity formation task is required just at a time when self-esteem can plunge to low levels where depression and anxiety may even create suicidal thoughts. One of the most challenging tasks is the integration of the physical self into the emerging identity (Biddle, Fox and Boucher, 2000). The body, the way it looks and performs is central to identity formation as it provides the public display of the self in its interactions with the world (Biddle, 1977).

Self-esteem becomes increasingly important in adolescence when preoccupation with one's self-image increases. Self-esteem becomes more vulnerable and peer approval more critical. Self-esteem however does develop over the course of adolescence (Hart, Fegley and Brengelman, 1993). Although adolescents make bids for autonomy from parents, they still want to remain connected and, thus, parent support continues to be critical.

Most young people have stable self-esteem but some show unstable fluctuations (Kernis and Waschull, 1996). Losing self-esteem leads to anger, hostility and other negative emotions. Self-esteem is not fixed for life, and significant changes in circumstances may be accompanied by changes in how students regard themselves. Change is most likely during times of transition, such as transferring from primary to secondary school, or school to higher education. A re-evaluation of self-esteem is more likely during such transitions because they bring changes in one's perceptions of competence, given the new developmental tasks to be mastered, the new groups with whom one compares oneself and the new areas that are seen as important.

Positive and negative esteem

Students with low self-esteem are often assumed to regard themselves as unlovable and generally useless. Although there may be a few who hate themselves, they are a small minority (Baumeister, 1993). Students with positive self-esteem have positive views about themselves but low self-esteem is not the opposite. Positive self-esteem is an unconditional feeling of regard for the self that does not depend on the perception that one has any particular positive qualities or is approved of by particular people. Students with positive self-esteem, however, do think they are good at most things, they want others to recognize their qualities and to achieve success.

Students with low self-esteem are not pathetic self-haters but are rather uncertain students who are neutral or non-committal about themselves. They are low in self-esteem only in comparison to the flattering way students with high self-esteem portray themselves. Low self-esteem may be better understood as the absence of positive views of self rather than the presence of negative views (Baumeister, 1993).

An understanding of the role of self-esteem requires consideration of stability as well as of level (Keegan *et al.*, 1995). Students with low self-esteem with the greatest emotional difficulties are those with low and unstable self-esteem (Keegan *et al.*, 1995). A lot of disconnected and/or controlling feedback from parents and teachers in early childhood has been found to promote an unstable self-esteem (Kernis and Waschull, 1996).

Self-esteem is perhaps more usefully considered in terms of a continuum of negative to positive esteem, as opposed to low to high esteem. These terms will be adopted throughout the text.

Self-enhancement and protection

There is little difference between students with positive and negative esteem in their responses to feedback. Everyone prefers success and approval to failure and rejection. The difference is that students with positive esteem are more concerned with self-enhancement while negative esteem students are more concerned with self-protection. Positive self-esteem students behave in a self-aggrandizing way (Swann, 1996). Students with low self-esteem fear failure that outweighs the desire for success, resulting in cautious behaviour. Their self-protection orientation inclines them towards low-risk safe situations. By rating the self negatively, students can reduce the damage of any negative evaluations, rejection or failure (Epstein, 1992). A similar process drives those people who invest a lot of their resources in insurance, reducing their quality of life but providing great security.

Students with negative self-esteem lack a clear, consistent and unified understanding of who they are and they have fewer definite beliefs about what they are like than others. This leaves them at the mercy of events resulting in their self-conceptions changing from day to day (Kernis *et al.*, 1995). Students with positive self-esteem can draw on their extensive self-knowledge to manage their lives more effectively. They focus on their good points and seek to cultivate them so as to stand out. A history of success in several domains helps develop a more complex self.

Students with negative self-esteem appear concerned with remedying their deficiencies in order to reach a passable level of performance and protect themselves against further humiliating failures. Such students, like those who keep their hood up in class, or insist on wearing a cap or who cannot cope with praise, are usually concerned with protecting their 'private' esteem, while self-enhancers are more concerned with enhancing their 'public' esteem. Teachers who insist they take off their cap cannot realize how intrusive that is. It is important to recognize that even when students use self-defeating strategies, such as withholding effort, cheating or procrastination, their goal is to protect their self-esteem (Raffini, 1993).

Lacking firm self-knowledge, students with negative esteem may fall into various traps such as setting inappropriate goals, starting things that are too difficult to achieve or too easy to be worth bothering about. This uncertainty leaves them at the mercy of feedback. Students with positive self-esteem can ignore criticism because they feel certain that it does not describe them correctly.

Students can become trapped by negative self-esteem when they are unable to minimize the importance of their weaknesses. Normally students support favourable views of themselves by using biases and defences to interpret events in ways that favour them (Taylor, 1990). These positive illusions are an integral part of adjustment. Students with negative self-esteem seem to lack these self-serving distortions and prefer to see themselves in an accurate way and so protect themselves against loss and disappointment. We feel the way we think.

Negative self-esteem students may even prefer negative feedback to confirm their current level of esteem. Most people seek self-verification and want to be given information to confirm who they think they are even if they do not think much of themselves. People act in such a way as to elicit their preferred feedback. Flattering feedback may trigger a conflict between a desire to gain esteem and a sceptical distrust mixed with a reluctance to accept the risks of a positive self-image. Negative self-esteem can thus become self-perpetuating.

Contingent self-esteem

Contingent self-esteem is different from negative self-esteem. Conditionality of acceptance is the extent to which a student feels that acceptance is forthcoming only if certain standards are met. This is in contrast to unconditional positive regard where the child is valued for who he or she is, not for whether he or she fulfils the expectations of others (Rogers, 1961). Conditional acceptance, even with relatively high levels of support, undermines self-esteem because it does not signify approval of the self but, rather, specifies what one has to do to be given worth (Kamins and Dweck, 2000). As such, it is experienced as controlling rather than affirming.

For some students, their self-esteem is reliant upon the approval of others. Extreme forms of contingent esteem are seen in people who are constantly apologetic or who are always asking 'if that's alright' or who ingratiate themselves with other people. For others their feelings of worth have been internalized. The latter group are not dependent on others to sustain a sense of self-esteem and such autonomy, perhaps, is the basis for 'true' self-esteem. A distinction needs to be made between true self-esteem and insecure, defensive narcissism (Rogers, 1961). Contingent esteem is dependent on living up to some controlling standard, for example parental expectations or comparison with older siblings (Burhans and Dweck, 1995). Indeed, given the conditional status of many relationships, perhaps the ebb and flow generated by this more fragile contingent self-esteem is common and it is the minority who have true and robust self-esteem. Robust self-esteem, like a robust argument can withstand attack and criticism. Those with true esteem will be less put off by failure, criticism and rejection, and be more accepting of both self and others.

The flawed belief that causes contingent low self-esteem is of not being worthwhile, a feeling usually caused by constant disapproval or early rejection. This belief is based on the questionable assumption that worth is a quality we either have or we do not have (Burns, 1993). We all have strengths and weaknesses, and specific skills can have more or less worth. Individuals, however, should not be thought of as having more or less worth.

Teachers and schools may reinforce contingent self-esteem by, for example, setting up competitive situations where only the successful will be valued or by stressing the importance of academic achievement as the main, or indeed sole, criterion of worth. The more pressure on schools to produce high-achieving students the more conditional teachers may become. Feedback that is repeatedly directed at the child as a whole, involving personalized labels such as 'you are a poor speller' or 'you are a pest', rather than focused on the piece of work or particular behaviour, imply contingent regard. Even when their failure is quite specific, students with contingent self-esteem may draw a negative conclusion about their entire worth and engage in global self-blame.

Contingent self-esteem can lead to students being ego-involved in dutifully achieving learning outcomes (Ryan, 1982) and to a tendency to invest too much of their self-esteem in everyday school activities. It tends to be associated with a kind of narcissism that keeps one anxiously absorbed in one's own agenda. For some students their self-esteem is a precious and fragile commodity, and this vulnerability makes them very 'touchy'. Contingent self-esteem often triggers social comparison because, to the extent that one has to live up to others' standards, one is likely to check this out in terms of how one measures up to others.

Is high self-esteem such a good thing?

A widely and long-held assumption in education and society as a whole has been that low self-esteem is one of the most significant roots of underachievement, disaffection and anti-social behaviour. While it has been found to be a risk factor for private difficulties such as suicide, depression, teenage pregnancy and victimization, there is little evidence for the idea that it is a risk factor for underachievement (Baumeister, Smart and Boden, 1996). The idea that high self-esteem is both an asset to society and an individual right has had a major impact on education and has led to an explosion in self-help manuals (Emler, 2001). It has led to the popular belief that an important function of schools should be to maintain high esteem for all students and to take steps to boost under-achieving or problem students' self-esteem. The recent rise in depressive illnesses among young people has been thought by some to be partly caused by the 'self-esteem move-ment', which has persuaded some young people that self-esteem is sufficient for success, but are then discouraged when success does not occur (Rayner and Montague, 2000).

High self-esteem may be desirable but most of its benefits may accrue to the individual, while it might even cause some problems to everyone else (Swann, 1996). The term has acquired positive connotations but there are many synonyms that are more mixed in tone including egotism, ego-trip, conceit, showing off, self-importance, narcissism, prima donna. As the Irish proverb warns, 'walk easy when your cup is full'.

High self-esteem is perhaps not always such a good thing. It would suggest that one has achieved as much as possible, a complacent conclusion that is incompatible with a mas-tery mindset that realizes one can always improve. High self-esteem is not always helpful in promoting achievement as it may lead to excessive and unrealistically high risks and goals (Baumeister, 1993).

Another common assumption is that violence is caused by low self-esteem, but recent research suggests that violence can be a result of threatened egotism (Baumeister, Smart and Boden, 1996; Bushman and Baumeister, 1998). People with negative feelings about themselves treat themselves badly but they do not usually treat others badly. Unstable high self-esteem has been found to be associated with high levels of aggression (Kernis, Granneman and Barclay, 1989). High self-esteem can result from 'successful' delinquent behaviour (Hughes, Cavell and Grossman, 1997).

Students with high but unstable self-esteem share many similarities with those with con-tingent self-esteem, such as their ego involvement or touchiness. A bully, for example, often has an insecure but inflated view of his or her self. Feeling that he or she may lose esteem at any moment, the bully responds jealously, even violently, to a potential threat. People whose high self-esteem is inflated or unstable may be sensitive to negative feed-back and may respond with hostility often in a way that is out of proportion with the threat. Some students who have an aggressive and challenging attitude towards teachers may very well have such high esteem.

Others with high self-esteem and overconfidence tend to think they are invulnerable, often act with bravado and think rules are not for them, for example surgeons in hospi-tals who do not bother to comply with hygiene regulations. People with high self-esteem have also been found to be more apt to drink and drive, drive over the speed limit, to rationalize the health risks of smoking and underestimate their chances of getting pregnant (Emler, 2002).

High self-esteem has also been linked with greater hostility to out-groups. People with high esteem create less fortunate others with whom they can compare favourably (Gibbons and McCoy, 1991), and 'put down' out-group members, especially when their own group has been criticized (Crocker and Major, 1987). In its most extreme form high self-esteem is known as narcissistic personality disorder, with fantasies of grandeur and a pumped up sense of self. Such people are insensitive to the needs and feelings of others and exploit others for their own purposes (Baumeister, 1993). High esteem is perhaps problematic because it is often contingent or inflated and, therefore, fragile and volatile.

Diagram 5.1 summarizes the major self-esteem dimensions and categories discussed in this section.

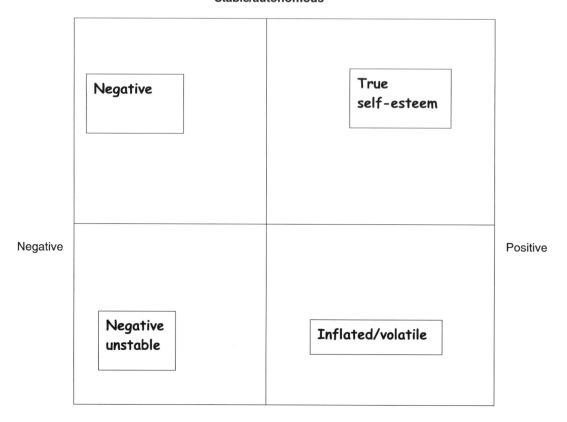

Diagram 5.1 ■ The self-esteem dimensions

The Puzzle of Self-esteem

Our fascination with self-esteem is understandable but our understanding is confused particularly with regard to its role in motivating learning. The role of self-esteem is more complex than we usually assume (Tyler and Kramer, 1999). The interplay between esteem and motivation is like the relationship between wealth and happiness; not having wealth may make you unhappy, but having it does not guarantee happiness. Positive esteem does not guarantee high motivation, neither is it essential for self-motivation. Most people tend to evaluate themselves positively, focus on their strengths, exaggerate their part in any success and ignore their weaknesses (Snyder *et al.*, 1983; Taylor, 1990) but not everyone is positively motivated to learn.

Self-esteem is often thought of as something teachers can nurture in students by, for example, praising their good features and protecting them from their deficiencies. But this may just be pretending their difficulties do not exist and will not help them cope with setbacks. Focusing on supporting self-esteem may only offer the student ways to avoid facing up to, and learning from, their problems and mistakes.

Damage to self-esteem has adverse effects on everyone and we all want to avoid this. Trying to raise students' self-esteem directly, however, may have limited success as this ignores the fact that many of our feelings about our selves come from what we do rather than cause us to do it (Kernis, 1995).

There are some students who rely to some extent on teachers for their esteem, particularly those with more fragile self-esteem. When teachers do nurture student self-esteem, however, it will tend to be of a contingent quality as the teacher–student relationship is a conditional one that is, by its nature, based on acceptance that can be withdrawn at any time. This relationship also has quite specific boundaries within which the teacher must operate.

We usually think of boosting self-esteem as the way to produce confident students. Schools, however, cannot directly influence esteem as readily as we think. For a start this assumes teachers are in control of their own self-esteem. Self-esteem is something students determine for themselves and is shaped by factors often unknown to and out of the control of teachers, namely, whatever is really valued by students, including for example their physical appearance or peer group acceptance.

The largest single source of variations in self-esteem is genetic, at least one-third of the variation may be attributable to this single factor (Kendler, Gardner and Prescott, 1998). This, however, means that most of the differences between students' self-esteem are due to the things that happen to them in their lives. Next in importance comes parental impact. Four qualities of parental treatment of children are crucial to self-esteem (Coopersmith, 1967): acceptance, clear standards of expected behaviour, control based on explanation rather than coercion and participation in family decision-making. A more recent review (Feiring and Taska, 1996) singled out acceptance as the key factor. Self-esteem does eventually become more aligned with peer approval but parents' opinions remain significant well into the adolescent and, even, adult years. Beyond the parental effect, little else has been found to modify the opinion of the self (Emler, 2002).

While teachers can allocate worth to students, they cannot give students true self-esteem. Teachers are not often significant figures in students' lives. This is not to suggest that teachers are not powerful influences on students. Students place a great amount of trust in their teachers. Teachers can think they have little influence, but they often fail to grasp this apparent contradiction and do not fully realize what power they do have over students. Hence the odd throwaway remark from a teacher that leaves the student distressed. This distress is sometimes caused by clumsy attempts at humour at the expense of the student through, for example, personalized and sometimes offensive nicknames. Ironically the more challenging the student, the more frustrated and disempowered the teacher feels, the more desensitized the teacher is likely to become to their power to upset students.

It may, in fact, be the case that teachers can more readily damage student self-esteem than build it, particularly for students who come to school with an already fragile esteem. Like trust or reputation, self-esteem takes a long time to develop but can be quickly demolished. Personalized disapproval, for example, has been found to be more likely to lower self-esteem than inclusion or acceptance is to raise it (Terdal and Leary, 1991).

Fortunately it is easy to avoid damaging student self-esteem by refraining from destructive personal attacks such as judgemental criticism and personalized blame, capricious overcontrolling or unfair discipline, and neglect and disinterest. Further good news is that negative self-esteem is not as big a barrier to confident learning as we think. Girls, for example, generally are thought to have less positive self-esteem than boys, yet generally show more positive motivation for learning (King, *et al.*, 1999). Research has consistently found only a small association between academic achievement and self-esteem (Hoge, Smit and Crist, 1995). The even better news is that schools can influence the key mindsets that shape student confidence and self-motivation to learn. Self-esteem tends to follow from more than cause achievement.

Where our confusion about self-esteem has led us

There are a number of unhelpful practices that follow from our confused ideas about self-esteem.

Most teachers think that telling students how clever they are builds their confidence. Such praise for ability, however, encourages students to concentrate on showing their ability rather than on learning. They may then also put failure down to ability. It may instil the belief that ability is something they cannot change. Confidence can crumble if students have this fixed idea of ability, because no matter how confident, failure will mean low ability. A more robust confidence is nurtured in classrooms that convey that ability can grow, that students will progress if they apply themselves and use the right approaches. Even students with low confidence but who think of ability as changeable cope better with setbacks than confident students with fixed ability ideas (Dweck, 2000).

Another common mistake is for teachers to praise unrealistically high ambitions and, so, unwittingly reinforce goals that are destined to lead to disappointment. It is perhaps more helpful to focus praise upon an accurate match between students' aspirations and their current skill level.

The confusion is further reflected in schools' struggle between giving students honest feedback and maintaining their self-esteem. When teachers give unsolicited help or sympathy they soften the blow of failure to protect student esteem but may suggest to the student he or she has low ability. A well-chosen and carefully delivered criticism can communicate high expectations, while indiscriminate praise for easy success can be meaningless and convey disinterest. As long as students know their worth is secure they will absorb accurate feedback in relation to what they do. Comments about their individual qualities, however, are more threatening to student self-esteem.

A Better Way to Build Confidence

Esteem-building approaches are laudable but in isolation will not nurture confident learners. This requires attention to be focused on specific aspects of competency that are important to the student rather than vague attempts to make students feel good about themselves. Self-esteem can only result from competencies in real-life situations, not from praise and confidence-building (Seligman, 1998). Confidence-building teachers instil the beliefs that ability is not fixed and that there are many ways to succeed. They treat mistakes as essential steps to efficacy by linking failure to factors that students can repair. Confidence depends less on actual achievement than on the relationship between achievement and aspirations. Motivating teachers encourage an accurate match between students' aspirations and their current skills level. They praise effort and strategy use in order to help students focus on the process of their work, make them feel responsible for success and emphasize the possibility of improvement. This encourages students to concentrate on learning rather than displaying ability, and to put progress down to effort. Most important of all, they stress personal rather than normative success, and so encourage a mastery attitude to achievement.

The twin-track approach to confident students involves teaching them to think of their ability as changeable and so lead them to adopt a mastery mindset and to help them make sense of progress in a way that builds their competence beliefs. Not every student can be the best, but they can all be high in mastery attitudes to achievement. Each of the four motivation mindsets most likely impact on the same neural pathways to the left prefrontal cortex that generates confidence (Davidson, Putnam and Larson, 2000). The real 'feel-good' mindset is self-efficacy in goal achievement – the 'SEGA' factor.

We motivate ourselves by thinking we can achieve our goals by our own skills and actions (Bandura, 1997). A clear relationship has been found between self-efficacy beliefs and academic productivity (Tuckman and Sexton, 1990). Developing a competency of any kind strengthens the sense of self-efficacy making a person more willing to take risks and to seek out challenges (Seligman *et al.*, 1995). Surmounting challenges, in turn, increases this sense of self-efficacy, an attitude that allows students to make the best use of whatever skills they have. Part-time or voluntary work and developing competencies in leisure and cultural pursuits all help the promotion of self-efficacy through the capacity of the student to exert agency over their environment (Gilligan, 2001). Students with a high sense of competency are more likely to choose difficult tasks, expend greater effort, persist longer, apply appropriate problem-solving strategies and have less fear and anxiety regarding tasks.

Self-efficacy has been found to exert its influence on achievement through student goals. Hence, belief in yourself appears to influence goals for which you strive (Dweck, 1992; Locke and Latham, 1990). In a learning situation we are more likely to ask, 'will I be any good at this?' than 'how do I feel about myself?'

Self-efficacy in fulfilling goals that help us realize important aspects of our ideal self is particularly useful in generating positive feelings about the self. The value of an educational experience is the extent to which it fulfils the student's goals. Feelings towards goal attainment are determined by whether or not our actual self matches our desired self. When we fulfil the goals about who we ideally want to be we get a 'buzz', a 'spring in our step' and feel good. Such positive emotions are the neon lights for growth that mobilize creative thinking. It is even better if our goals are achieved in the context of the highest possible challenge and skill level. Just having high efficacy, however, is not enough to ensure true self-esteem and intrinsic motivation; these efficacy beliefs must be accompanied by a sense of autonomy (Deci and Ryan, 1995; Ryan, 1993) to create an optimal level of self-motivation.

When the SEGA state is achieved the brain's neurotransmitters work in unison to produce the feel-good condition. Testosterone rises to keep us focused. Adrenalin floods through our blood stream to keep us alert and speed our recovery. Dopamine stimulates our brain's pleasure centre to give a profound sense of well-being as endorphins rush through the body producing the body's natural high (Winston, 2002).

How the Mindsets Work Together

While teachers may not be able to impact directly on student self-esteem, they can influence the four motivation mindsets. Teachers can, for example, encourage students to think of ability as changeable and encourage them to adopt a mastery attitude and to make optimistic explanations for their success that help build their confidence. Students interpret their progress by assimilating into their own way of thinking the reasons that teachers attribute to their progress. These factors determine student self-determination and, subsequently, contribute to self-esteem that in turn further influences their ideas about ability, attributions, achievement attitudes and self-efficacy. These key factors are illustrated in Diagram 5.2.

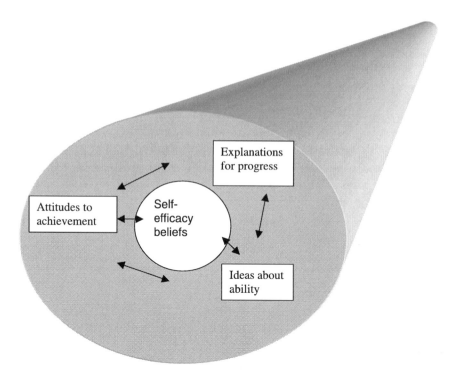

Diagram 5.2 ■ The motivation mindsets

The motivation mindsets have reciprocal influences on one another. The causal chain between them can go in either direction, as all four mindsets are intertwined. Students' ideas about ability, explanations of progress, attitudes towards achievement and self-competency beliefs all interact to create their motivation profile and help shape their self-determination and self-esteem, which in turn impacts on their mindsets. However, ideas about the nature of ability will certainly affect attitudes towards achievement and these, in turn, shape students' explanations of progress that influence self-efficacy beliefs. For example, those with a mastery mindset are likely to attribute success to internal, stable and controllable factors, particularly effort. Those with a performance mindset are more likely to use ability attributions.

The link between ideas about ability, achievement attitudes and subsequent response to setbacks is summarized in Diagram 5.3. Incremental ideas of ability are more likely to lead to a mastery mindset and a meaning system that links effort with progress and failure with insufficient effort (Molden and Dweck, 2000). This way of thinking is likely to encourage a mastery response to setbacks, challenges and failure. On the other hand, fixed ideas of ability are more likely to lead to a performance mindset and a meaning system that links both effort and failure with low ability. This way of thinking is likely to encourage an avoidance response to setbacks, challenges and failure, in terms of either a self-protective or helpless response.

Ideas about → ability	Achievement → attitudes	Meaning system →	Response to setback
Incremental	Mastery	Effort = progress Failure = not enough effort	Perseverance
Entity	Performance	Effort = low ability Failure = low ability	Self-protection or helplessness

Diagram 5.3 ■ How ideas about ability and achievement attitudes shape response to setbacks

The Role of Self-esteem in Motivating Learning

Current theories of motivation recognize the centrality of the self. Consequently, feelings about the self provide an important backdrop to self-motivation. We may achieve a deeper understanding of the role of self-esteem in motivating learning by considering its connections with the four mindsets. The primary cause of educational disaffection is not negative self-esteem but a lethal cocktail of fixed ability ideas, pessimistic explanations of progress, a strong performance attitude and low competency beliefs.

Students with contingent self-esteem may be more likely to have fixed ideas about ability and a performance attitude to achievement (Kamins and Dweck, 1998). Students with positive self-esteem will tend to be optimistic and put down failure to transient events over which they feel they have some control and to attribute success to internal stable characteristics. They will certainly be less put off by failure and cope well with obstacles, and so enjoy mastery self-referenced ratings of progress that in turn are more likely to maintain positive self-esteem (Kavussanu and Harnisch, 2000). If a person has a mastery attitude and is not progressing as well as others he or she can still have positive self-esteem, unlike someone with a performance attitude who will maintain positive esteem only if he or she is doing well. Because it is not possible for all students to be the best, encouraging students to concentrate on achieving their personal best will be important for student self-esteem.

Some students with negative self-esteem attribute success to luck and failure to personal characteristics that they consider hard to change, leading to an expectation of failure and a sense of helplessness.

This overview suggests that thinking about self-esteem should be two-tiered. First, there is the permeating process (like sunshine) of global self-esteem that filters our thinking and feeling about our self. Secondly, there is the contextual appraisal of specific capability (like the weather conditions on the ground). Permeating self-esteem, like the sun is a constant. Sometimes however we lose sight of the sun when it is behind cloud cover, just as we meet setbacks or failure. Those with robust self-esteem know the sun is still there and so their self-esteem is not undermined. Those with fragile esteem worry that it has permanently gone. They lose their positive feelings of self-esteem until the next successful experience or burst of sunshine.

Self-esteem, like sunshine, is a bonus but not essential, and it will be more productive for teachers to focus on what they can most readily effect, that is, the motivation mindsets.

The dynamic interplay between self-efficacy and self-esteem is like that between fitness and health. Both efficacy and fitness can fluctuate and can also be built up quickly in small steps. Just as fitness can contribute to, and be enhanced by, good health, so self-efficacy contributes to, and is enhanced by, positive self-esteem. The positive conclusion drawn here is that teachers can readily impact on the malleable mindsets that shape self-motivation and, in turn, nurture positive self-esteem.

Helpful and unhelpful motivational profiles

Many able students underachieve while many who are seen as less able end up achieving more than predicted. What actually determines achievement? A crucial factor is students' ability to cope with challenges and setbacks. Some students love challenges, are willing to take risks and thrive when they hit obstacles. These students may not start out being highly skilled, but they become so over time. The students who are afraid of challenges and avoid risks and failure gradually fall behind.

High achievers may appear to be able to perform skills effortlessly but this apparent ease is due to great effort (Howe, 1999). There is no short cut to high achievement. High achievers have a capacity to work very hard and show a determined single-mindedness and strong commitment to their activities. They are keen to achieve success. They are very sure about what they want to do and have a clear and strong sense of direction as well as an unusual level of curiosity. They put down their success to hard work as well as their skills that they know they can control, and so are high in self-efficacy beliefs. They have incremental ideas about ability and adopt a mastery attitude to achievement. Consequently, they enjoy high intrinsic motivation and are deeply absorbed in tasks, cope well with failure and are able to keep persisting no matter how frustrating the task.

The motivation profile of disengaged students provides a stark contrast. They have a complex set of negative ideas about themselves within the learning context. They may have a low need for achievement and be interested only in basic needs. Some disengaged students may be motivated by fear of failure and may have adopted a passive helplessness or developed self-protective strategies. A performance attitude and beliefs about the fixed nature of ability may exacerbate these features. The primary cause of educational disaffection is repeatedly putting failure down to stable, personal, uncontrollable and global factors that suggest failure is inevitable. This leads to low self-efficacy beliefs and low expectations. Students with a lethal cocktail of such pessimistic explanations of progress, fixed ability ideas, a strong performance attitude and low competency beliefs are especially vulnerable to a spiral of failure avoidance and demotivation.

It is difficult for them to escape from this spiral without a dramatic change in the learning context. All students, however, can rediscover an interest in learning, no matter how demotivated they have become, as long as they are matched to their optimal learning context.

The Complete Motivation Model

The motivation mindsets and self-esteem can now be added to the drivers outlined earlier to complete the motivation model (Diagram 5.4).

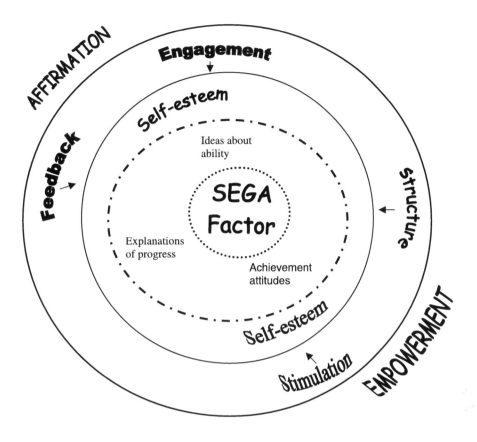

Diagram 5.4 ■ The motivation model

6 The Power of Learning Goals

This chapter looks at the important role played by goals, their benefits and key features.

Learning goals are targets to aim for and standards for evaluating student performance. When students set goals for themselves they act as representations of their future and, if they matter to them and are seen as attainable, they will be powerful motivators (Ames and Archer, 1988; Klein *et al.,* 1999; Nuttin and Lens, 1985). Future goals help both to structure and energize student behaviour. The very process of working towards valued goals enhances student well-being. Successful self-determination is a process of identifying goals, pursuing and attaining them, then seeking other goals.

The Benefits of Learning Goals

Some students perform better than others of similar ability often because they have different goals (Locke and Latham, 1990). Success-orientated students aspire to complex goals and learn to create small steps or stepping stones so that they are able to move from one to another (De Volder and Lens, 1982). Setting a goal demonstrates an intention to achieve and triggers learning. It also directs the student's activities towards the goal and offers an opportunity to experience success. The brain motivates us by carrying an image of where we want to go and how we will feel when we get there. Imagining something in great detail can activate the same brain cells involved in the actual activity (Kreiman, Koch and Fried, 2000). Students with a clear goal, for example identified through the process of target-setting, experience a sense of self-efficacy for attaining it and will continue to engage in activities they believe will lead to goal attainment. Competency beliefs are increased as they see goal progress that conveys they are becoming skilful. The greater the feeling of progress the greater the sense of control and confidence.

The important features of learning goals

The motivational benefits of goals depend on the properties of proximity, specificity, difficulty and how they are assigned (Ames, 1992).

Close-at-hand goals are more encouraging than distant goals because it is easier to judge progress towards them. The clearer, more concrete and observable the goal, the easier will it be to know what progress is being made. The more specific the goal, the clearer the benchmark and also the effort needed. Given enough ability and commitment, the harder and more specific the goal the better. Harder goals lead to better performance, although the relation may level off at levels of difficulty beyond the individual's ability. Specific and difficult goals lead to better performance than vague and global goals such as doing one's best. Students operating with do-your-best goals can use different standards to evaluate their performance which results in some being satisfied with low standards. In contrast, those operating under specific and difficult goals have a high standard on which to focus and by which to assess their performance.

Goals that are given with a clear rationale tend to be motivating. If the goals are negotiated, they will enable a greater sense of autonomy. Having children assist in defining goals increases the probability that they will understand and want to reach them.

Self-referring goals have the advantage of being 'absolute' in nature, unlike goals that involve comparison with peers. In the latter the measure of success is constantly changing and depends not only on how well the individual does, but also on how others do, something over which the individual has little control (Wiggins, 1989). When students are held to a well-defined standard of their own rather than expected to out perform others, failure tends to motivate them to try harder (Kennedy and Willcutt, 1964). Absolute goals also provide built-in criteria for gauging one's progress and for judging when one's work is finished.

Realistic goals

Students' judgements and feelings about success or failure depend less on their actual performance than on the relationship between their performance and their aspirations. Doing well depends as much on students choosing a realistic level of challenge as it does on ability. Accurate self-knowledge lets individuals credit their talents fairly as well as recognise their shortcomings. Students need to make realistic judgements about their own capacity relative to the demands of the task.

Some factors however can promote inappropriate goal choice including low teacher expectations, teacher preferences for superior achievement and the tendency for students to model themselves on high achieving students. Some students, particularly those with high self-esteem (Baumeister, Heatherton and Rice, 1993), can hold unrealistically high expectations. Teachers can mistakenly praise such aspirations as evidence of student willingness to try hard and so, unwittingly, may reinforce goals that are destined to lead to disappointment. In these circumstances it is perhaps more helpful to try to encourage students to match their aspirations with their current skills.

Challenge is not always as positive as we assume in this age of high achievement, and teachers need to try to find a realistic balance between low expectations and excessive off-putting challenges.

Goal-setting and persistence

Students take control of their successes and failures when they set their own goals and alter them as necessary. Goal-setting and persistence are affected by many factors, including the perceived possibility of attaining the goal, the importance or desirability of the goal, the appropriateness or legitimacy of the goal and peer support (Ames, 1992). The skills of goal-setting, however, need to be explicitly taught. Although students might consider a goal as desirable and possible to achieve, there is still a choice they have to make, reflecting their commitment to the goal. Personal factors, most importantly previous performance and their skill level, will influence their commitment. Self-efficacy is one of the most important influences on personal goal-setting (Bandura, 1989). Personal beliefs about the goal, which may be based on interest, utility or importance, can influence goal choice and commitment. Mood also affects goal choice.

Role models, competition and pressure can increase the perceived importance of a goal. Group norms seem to have a positive effect on goal-setting. Positive role-modelling of goal-setting makes individuals set higher goals for themselves (Roeser, Midgley and Urdan, 1996). Students will be more committed to the goals when the authority figure is seen as supportive, trustworthy, knowledgeable and likeable, gives a convincing rationale for the goal and exerts reasonable pressure.

Social goals

Most students value their social goals more highly than learning goals, particularly peer-orientated goals. We all know the best parts of conferences are the informal contacts at the coffee breaks. The social aspects of school may be more important than the curriculum, for example when students are deciding whether or not to stay on at school (Mangan, Adnett and Davis, 2001). School adjustment requires the pursuit of multiple and often complementary social and academic goals (Juvonen and Wentzel, 1996). Students are motivated to achieve a range of social goals, such as helping others, pleasing adults, forming friendships, making relationships with their teachers, achieving a sense of belonging, developing their social identity and accessing social approval. These, in turn, enhance a sense of social competence and provide social contexts that motivate academic achievement. How young people are regarded by their peers is a better long-term predictor of well-being than academic achievements, IQ scores, teachers' ratings or absenteeism (Cassidy and Asher, 1992; Cowen, 1973). Classmates are potential friends but also crucial reference groups that stimulate intense comparison.

Western culture promotes the development of independence and autonomy in males and interdependence and relatedness in females. Consequently, girls are more likely to define themselves on the basis of their relationships and group membership (Cross and Madson, 1997). In contrast boys' self-definition will be based on their unique features and the importance of distinguishing themselves from others. While males also seek relationships, these relationships often reflect individualistic goals.

Peer acceptance

Peer acceptance is a major issue for young people and may even be as important if not more important than friendships (Juvonen and Wentzel, 1996). While they are seeking autonomy and separation from their parents they also want to be the same as everyone else. The peer group is a vital source of social comparison as well as of guidance on how to behave and what to think.

Break time may be one of the few times during the school day when students can interact with peers on their own terms and practise important social skills (Pellegrini and Blatchford, 2000)). Break time is spent in co-operative interaction, involving peer-regulated games. Playground games are particularly important at the start of the year, when peers do not know each other very well. Games play an important role for young children by providing a scaffold through which unacquainted students can interact. Unfamiliar students use shared knowledge of a game as an initial basis for mixing. Games also support new social contacts. Entering into and suggesting games provide the opening for new relationships. After the initiation phase, students then use games to consolidate existing groups and friendships.

Peer relations, as reflected by playground behaviour, predict adjustment to school more generally. The efficacy that students experience at playground games during their first years of schooling transfers to more general feelings of competence in school.

Feelings about goals

One of the purposes of our emotions is to tell us the consequences of our actions (Carver and Scheier, 1998). Feelings such as pride and shame also tell us about our status within groups (Lewis, *et al.*, 2000). Feelings are the result not only of the attainment of goals, but also of the rate of progress towards our goals. The intensity function of motivation, that is, the level of enthusiasm, is determined by our emotions which are, in turn, affected by our rate of progress. Negative feelings reflect a disappointing rate of progress, indicating a problem; things are not moving forward fast enough. Positive feelings result when things are going well or better than expected. Positive feelings may cause complacency, as shown in the ebb and flow of sports competitions. Feelings operate like the cruise control of a car (Carver and Scheier, 1998). If you are going too slowly towards your goal, negative affect leads to more effort. Going fast creates positive affect that leads to coasting. Shifts in rate of progress can be gradual or abrupt. Abrupt progress causes a rush of exhilaration, while abrupt stalling leads to 'that sinking feeling'. If progress slows just before goal attainment, we sometimes experience a feeling of 'anti-climax'.

As discussed earlier, we have two main types of goals. The first is concerned with moving towards our ideal self. The second moves us towards our 'ought' self. Achieving a goal with an ideal self-focus (for example, the lead role in the school show) leads to happiness.

When we fulfil our goals concerning the kind of person we want to be we feel elation. Not achieving such a goal leaves us feeling dejected. Achieving an 'ought' goal (for example, visiting an elderly parent or sending Christmas cards) makes us feel relieved, while failure makes us feel agitated. The interplay between our 'ought' and 'ideal' goals is similar to that between the concepts of responsibilities and rights.

Part III

The Drivers in Action

7 Engagement – Creating Learning Relationships

This chapter outlines the ways teachers, through the engagement driver and each of its gears, let students know how they are valued. This is achieved through their attitudes and expectations, how they label students, their use of competition and co-operation, and how they group students.

What is Engagement?

To get to know the student is the first goal of motivation. Engagement refers to the quality of the relationship between teacher and students and between peers. The need to belong to a community of learners is a basic motivator for students (Baumeister and Leary, 1995). Engagement is the term often used to describe students' general involvement with learning. The focus of the engagement driver is narrowed to social and emotional engagement. The teacher's desire to understand and get to know students is communicated by the dedication of resources, distribution of teacher time and availability when needed. The affect surrounding the engagement is important. Teachers' emotions are contagious and will be most helpful when they create resonance and positive feelings. The degree of sensitivity with which teachers tune into students' concerns shapes the extent to which students feel their needs are being met. The teacher qualities that matters to students are as much about how they are treated as how they are taught (Rudduck, 1998).

Inter-subjectivity is the degree of common understanding between the teacher and student (Bruner, 1996). Some teachers see students as quite different from themselves, like lion trainers see lions. Others, in contrast, apply the same ideas to themselves as they apply to their students and, so, are more able to grasp how students view the learning context.

Students discover what teachers think of them by observing their behaviour towards them. They will notice subtle details, for example when the teacher takes a greater interest in other students. Many students dislike teachers who favour high fliers at the expense of slower students. They particularly dislike teachers who do not bother to learn their names. If the teacher does not like them students are unlikely to be interested in the subject taught.

Engagement is transmitted through the classroom climate. Climate is hard to define, less difficult to describe but easy to experience. Individual classroom climates contribute to, and are shaped by, the school culture that provides the guiding beliefs that pervade a school and the spirit that motivates ideas and practices. Classroom mood is a state of readiness to experience certain emotions (Lewis, Amini and Lannon, 2000). Every detail of teacher attitudes, expectations and behaviour contribute to the establishment of a motivating climate in which the teacher fosters positive attitudes towards self-improvement.

Of great importance to the classroom climate is the so-called 'hidden curriculum', the way the teacher's actions, however trivial, telegraph information about their attitudes and expectations. Much of this communication may be unintended and serve to undermine the teacher's effectiveness. Non-verbal communication is the language of emotion and interpersonal relationships, and is perhaps even more important than speech in establishing rapport. Body language is now understood not just as an alternative to speech, but as part of a multi-channel communication system, giving the skilled communicator a range of tools through which to convey meaning (Bull, 2002).

Different attitude sets from teachers have been found to lead to different responses from students (Hargreaves, 1975). Some teachers seem to bring out the worst in some students and amplify their problems, while others lead to the same students presenting relatively few problems.

Teacher attitudes and expectations – reverse gear

Central to the set of *rejecting* attitudes is the belief that students thought of as problematic do not want to work and will do anything to avoid it. Consequently, it is considered impossible to provide conditions under which they will work. Contact with these students is seen as a battle that must be won at all costs. If the teacher expects bad behaviour, he or she is more likely to look out for and then see it. Challenging students are regarded as anti-authority and determined non-conformists. They will be neglected in lessons and punished inconsistently, while students who conform will be given preferential treatment. Such students, predominantly boys, are expected to behave badly and, consequently, many pejorative comments will be made about them and negative labels ascribed to them. They will be referred to a higher authority as soon as they refuse to comply. Informal contact will be avoided and any signs of improvement will not be accepted as genuine. The underlying assumption is that these students are not to be trusted.

Some teachers deliberately provoke students by suggesting, for example: 'You have no chance of passing this exam, why are you taking this class?' One can only assume that they have been motivated by this themselves and so believe it to be effective. The intention of such teachers is to challenge the student to prove them wrong, to goad the student into action. This can indeed be effective in providing an additional spur to greater efforts, particularly with boys, who are more likely to respond to the challenge, or students with robust egos. Such 'scare tactics', however, have the great danger of being offputting for those students with vulnerable self-esteem and low self-efficacy, who believe what the teacher is saying and experience it as criticism. Like rote learning, it might work but it will never leave the student wanting more. Such negative feelings dampen the brain's capacity to focus on learning. Even for those who are motivated by it, such negative motivation often leaves a feeling of bitterness against the teacher, a hostility to learning and a damage to self-esteem. This kind of treatment inevitably encourages a *prove yourself* or *prove them wrong* mentality rather than an *improve yourself* attitude to achievement in students.

This style of interaction continues to be an endemic part of our culture, especially among males, illustrated for example by fathers berating their sons to greater efforts from the sidelines of the football or rugby pitch on a Saturday morning. Motivation by fear or intimidation may enhance short-term performance but it will not facilitate learning.

As well as *rejecting* attitudes, some teachers have neglecting attitudes and show little interest in particular students. Some students are made to feel invisible in their class. In other classes the students are not allowed to talk to each other, which makes it impossible for them to develop any co-operative work skills.

Teacher attitudes and expectations – first gear

An engaging classroom climate is more likely to foster a mastery attitude, when an emphasis is given to an 'improve yourself' rather than a 'prove yourself' approach to learning. A climate that focuses attention on skills related to individual standards will encourage a mastery attitude. A competitive climate will lead to thinking of ability as a native endowment and encourage a performance attitude.

Teachers can help to nurture feelings of engagement by:-

■ recognizing students' individual personalities
■ greeting each child by name

- knowing students by their competencies rather than their difficulties
- celebrating students' natural group role, such as the bossy or helping student
- letting each student have a share of the display area from time to time
- making sure all students are given recognition from time to time
- valuing all achievements
- talking about how students feel and what they think
- allowing students to express their opinions and concerns
- displaying pictures etc. which students bring from home
- showing an interest in students' lives within and outwith school
- sending notes home about specific achievements
- showing an interest in what they are interested in, finding out about their hobbies and any special talents
- attending events in which they are taking part, such as sport or music events.

Support and recognition is not dependent on performance, and students feel the teacher has regard for their worth irrespective of their performance. Spending time in this way is as important as preparing lessons and marking work. Such efforts produce a bank of positive feelings between the teacher and students that can be drawn upon in times of conflict (Covey, 1990). Some of these may be more appropriate and readily achieved in primary than secondary schools.

Teacher attitudes and expectations – second gear

In contrast, an *engaging* attitude set conveys that the teacher and students are involved in a shared quest. Each has a different role but shares a 'we're in this together and you can count on me to do my part' attitude. These attitudes are based on the belief that students really want to work. If they do not, the learning conditions must be at fault and the teacher is responsible for changing them. These attitudes lead to quite different teacher behaviours. Favouritism, and the implied rejection of others students, will be avoided; informal contact outside the classroom will be welcomed. Students will not be derogated in class or in the staffroom where the teacher will often speak up for them. The underlying assumption is that these students can be trusted and respected.

These teachers see behaviour problems as a natural part of growing up and an assertion of independence. They build in mechanisms to allow some student dissent. They realize that students taunting the teacher is often like a dog tugging at a shoe. Anyone who has played tug with a dog will know it is not the shoe it wants but the mutual tugging.

Labelling – reverse gear

Teachers, like students, have implicit beliefs about ability and personality that shape how they make sense of students' performance. Teachers with an entity view will assume a student's personality is unchangeable and will be more likely quickly to apply a global label to students, assuming a student's character can be displayed through a one-off incident (Chiu, Hong and Dweck, 1997; Levy, Stroessner and Dweck, 1998). They believe character is a fixed and unitary feature that consistently influences all behaviour.

Some teachers have a need for definite answers, based on their preference for certainty over ambiguity. This strong need for closure may lead to leaping to conclusions on little evidence, followed by a reluctance to entertain views that are different from their own. They have a tendency to 'seize' on closure quickly and then 'freeze' on their judgement (Kruglanski and Webster, 1996). Such teachers may process less information before coming to a conclusion and consider fewer interpretations of the information. They form impressions more quickly and rely more on stereotypes. Some teachers, for example, assume particular special educational needs labels 'explain' everything about a student.

Incremental teachers who think personality is more fluid and malleable are not so quick to jump to conclusions. They assume the student has potential to change and so see mis-behaviour or lack of application as something to be resolved.

Reputations, once acquired, are difficult to discard (Jussim, 1989; Rosenthal and Jacobsen, 1968). Some teachers tend to stereotype certain students with adverse reputations that can sour the classroom climate. Stereotyping aims to reduce the complex social world of schools and it is not surprising that some teachers stereotype their students as a way of managing this complexity. Conclusions however can be formed quickly and students resent such hasty opinions. If these opinions are communicated as explicit labels, they undermine students' identity and damage their motivation. Some teachers may make assumptions about a potentially difficult student on the basis of slender evidence such as staff gossip, perceived ability, bad experiences with the student's siblings or one particular incident. Students' appearance is a particularly powerful trigger, as illustrated by teachers who, for example, assume boys wearing earrings will be troublemakers.

Some teachers tend more than others to use trait category labels such as intelligent, reliable or honest when describing others, rather than use concrete situation-specific labels such as 'focused on their project', making the assumption that people are the same across different situations.

As well as the overt labelling processes there are also subtler processes such as when a student is never asked to contribute to discussions, answer a question or do jobs for the teacher. Four factors seem to determine the likelihood of a student behaving in accordance with a label; how often he or she is labelled, how important the teachers' opinions are to him or her, how many teachers are applying the label and how public it is. Labels, like expectations, are inevitable, and in fact essential for teachers' understanding of students. Labelling alone does not obviously create student alienation and students do not become deviant overnight.

The way students' learning difficulties are labelled can determine how students, parents and teachers make sense of and deal with their problems. Labels can lead to optimistic or pessimistic attitudes. Some labels are constructive, others are confining.

Labels can sometimes amplify students' difficulties into a negative identity by:

▓ attributing problems to controllable factors that suggest the problem is self-inflicted
▓ suggesting the difficulty is permanent
▓ suggesting the difficulty is global
▓ creating negative expectations
▓ discouraging the student to accept responsibility
▓ attributing difficulties to uncontrollable factors
▓ encouraging a fear-of-failure attitude.

Labelling – first gear

Labels, however, can also transform students' difficulties into a positive learning identity by:

▓ acknowledging and describing the origins of the problem
▓ allowing students to reframe their problems
▓ suggesting the difficulty is specific rather than global
▓ giving an explanation and, thereby, relief for student and parents
▓ enabling a greater and more objective understanding
▓ setting realistic expectations
▓ attributing progress to factors beyond the student's control and so evoking sympathy
▓ replacing unhelpful amplifying personalized labels such as 'pest'.

The damaging effects of negative teacher labelling can be minimized if:

■ teachers are aware of the labels they are using and how they are communicating them
■ teachers adopt a sceptical attitude to staffroom gossip, the reputation of certain students and the 'sibling phenomenon'
■ any signs of improvement are acknowledged and encouraged
■ the behaviour rather than the student is the focus.

Competition and co-operation – first gear

A competitive situation is a good way to provide stimulating challenges and enjoyable fun, particularly for boys. It offers great potential for team-building, a sense of belonging and of being valued within a group of peers who can be mutually supportive. The roots of the word 'compete' are the Latin *con petire*, which mean, 'to seek together'. What we seek is to do our best and this task is made easier when others stretch us. There is nothing more motivating than having a worthy opponent, as illustrated by famous lifelong rivalries such as between Picasso and Matisse. Competition can increase enjoyment and the perceived importance of a goal for confident students. It can help spark a new interest. It is also useful to improve performance in simple, mechanical or repetitive tasks.

Teachers, however, need to work hard to keep competition under control and to help students to keep it in perspective. It is most effective when teachers can make the starting point as equal as possible

Competition – reverse gear

Any advantage of the competitive edge disappears, however, when the task requires that students come up with the best ideas for solving novel or complex problems. When beating others becomes more important than performing as well as possible, enjoyment tends to disappear. We only want to compete when we have a strong chance of success, namely, when our competitors are on our level. Excessive competition reduces students' work rate, damages confidence and encourages timidity, especially among girls (Boggiano and Pittman, 1992; Kohn, 1986).

Competition can get out of hand and lead to excessive rivalry between individuals and groups. Pupils can be forced to learn to put up a front to cope with the threat. In these conditions it may damage their interests in the activity. Some pupils do not understand it or fail to keep it in perspective. In competition, the end product can become more important than the process.

Only certain students will be interested in competing, determined by among other things their attitudes to achievement. It can encourage students to strive for selfish goals and teaches that other students are obstacles to success. Teachers can encourage contingent self-esteem by setting up a competitive situation where only the winner will be valued. If students believe their worth as a person is reflected in how well they perform on competitive tests, test taking can cause great anxiety and block out what students know as well as lead to students adopting self-protective strategies. Competition decreases sharply the number who can succeed. Indeed, by its very nature, success for some must imply failure for others. Excessive competition tends to magnify the positive feeling of success, that is, pride, but also the negative side of failure, namely, shame which leads to cheating or opting out.

Competitive rewards threaten intrinsic motivation, as they tend to be unrelated to the process of learning itself. This is particularly problematic for insecure students with low skill levels.

Negative feedback from teachers is particularly off-putting where there is an emphasis on competition. Competition leads to an increase in students attending to what others are doing and to applying less effort to their own work. Comparative evaluation contributes to a negative climate for students who compare unfavourably – as seen in their poor self-evaluation, avoidance of risks, low interest level and superficial learning. In addition, peers usually share this low self-rating.

Perhaps the biggest drawback with competition is that the yardstick of progress is constantly changing, as it depends not only on how well the individual does but also on how others do. When students are held to their own standard, failure implies falling short of their goal and, so, tends to motivate them. Failure in competition, on the other hand, implies falling short as a person and, as such, can be discouraging. In competition one's work is never done. The structure that absolute standards provide is particularly important for insecure students who often think the worst of themselves, no matter how well they perform.

Co-operation – second gear

Teachers can discourage comparison between students by, for example, making instruction individualized by providing different activities simultaneously with materials varied in level and content. Opportunities can be given for students to work with peers in a variety of changing groups. Students can work individually on different tasks and participate in groups not necessarily defined by ability, so that perceptions of ability are made less salient to achievement. Students can be encouraged to give positive feedback to each other, take some responsibility for others' learning and so co-operate rather than compete. In such a climate students learn more readily with each other instead of against or apart from each other.

Co-operative group work offers the possibility for enhanced performance by students who seek social approval from their peers. When students co-operate they are less prone to make errors because they share information and act as monitors. When working toward a common goal, it is in everyone's interest to correct errors. An incentive structure can be used with each individual needing to make his or her best efforts for the group to succeed (Slavin, 1984). The contribution of each member needs to be clearly identifiable. Co-operative teams help motivate students when each member is given an opportunity to take responsibility for an activity that affects the entire team.

The teacher should reward those who are supportive to classmates. Any behaviours that support the group merit encouragement, particularly those defining the group's objectives and energizing the group toward these objectives. Models are important influences on self-efficacy, allowing observation of successful peers mastering the task.

Group norms have a very powerful influence on student behaviour and attitudes. Teachers can make all students feel part of one homogenous group, a group that sees itself as competent and hard-working. Ways of doing this include giving the class their own flag or anthem, a particular dress code, a special name or simply a common goal. Cohesive groups support each other, including even the slowest learner, and individual improvements can be seen as a triumph for the group.

Co-operation supports everybody's efforts to achieve and leads students to feel more positive about themselves, each other and the subject. An affirming climate is encouraged when each student recognizes the worth of the contribution of others.

Student grouping – reverse gear

Ability grouping has been associated with low self-esteem, low expectations and anti-school attitudes in the lower ability groups who are labelled and stigmatized by staff and other students (Boaler, 1997; Boaler, William and Brown, 2000). Streaming, in particular, is thought to polarize students' attitudes into pro- and anti-school. Students are sensitive to the effects of ability grouping, particularly how these highlight differences in ability (Ireson and Hallam, 2001). They are well aware of how and why they are grouped.

Communicating ability levels through grouping leads to teasing of both high- and low-ability students. Two parallel cultures can develop, one held by teachers and shared by some students in which high attainment is valued, the other where students prefer the middle sets because being 'average' offers a safe option from teasing, an opportunity to have fun and an enjoyable atmosphere which is not too pressurized or competitive.

The way in which students are evaluated is one of the most important factors affecting their motivation. Poor progress is most likely to damage motivation where there is public evaluation of ability or an emphasis on comparison. Ability grouping may magnify student's initial levels of engagement. Students in high-ability groups tend to be encouraged to work more independently and be more self-determining, and allowed more choice and responsibility. Low streams and sets tend to be more tightly structured and have fewer opportunities for independent learning and creativity. Here the priority is conforming to rules and expectations.

Individuals may not respond to groupings in the same way. Some students in the top sets find the pace too fast and dislike the competitiveness and overdemanding expectations. Others find the curriculum stimulating and the competition and high expectations motivating. Sets make classes more homogenous and allow more co-operation but evidence suggests that higher-ability groups are supportive, while lower-ability classes tend to be characterized by disharmony.

Student grouping – first gear

The values and attitudes of the school are crucial in mediating the effects of student groupings, particularly teachers' expectations, the extent of social mixing and the competitive ethos (Ireson and Hallam, 2001). If ability groupings are adopted, schools must keep groupings under constant review and ensure that movement between sets is possible.

The main potential danger of ability groupings on students' motivation will come from rigid groupings that signal ideas about fixed ability. Streaming may, in addition, communicate assumptions about global ability. Schools must be aware of the messages students pick up through groupings, about how they are valued, what school is for and how well they are doing. Schools must ensure that an emphasis on high attainment is not paramount, that the skills of all students are valued and that there are many ways to succeed. They need to monitor students' attitudes towards learning and levels of engagement. Schools in particular need ways of checking how the structures are impacting on the key motivation mindsets.

8 Structure – from Teacher Authority to Student Autonomy

This chapter considers the benefits provided by the structure driver that supplies the explicit information about how students will achieve the desired outcomes. It discusses how teacher authority needs to gradually be transformed through the use of the Structure gears to student autonomy.

What is Structure?

By clearly communicating goals and responding consistently, teachers provide the required level of structure that students need to ensure their security and well-being. Most students, like financial markets, hate uncertainty. Predictability (or predictive ability) lets students know what is coming next and helps develop a sense of control and trust. This is particularly important for emotionally vulnerable students.

For adults the very constraints of work have been found to make it satisfying (Juster, 1985). These include having to be at a given place at a particular time, deadlines for completed tasks, working towards some larger goal with others, with everyone having a specified role. All of this takes place in a routine way. Being compelled to take part seems to be a key factor in making work a source of well-being. Overcoming our resistance to complete tasks that are initially disliked gives a form of satisfaction that is hard to match. In leisure the freedom to create our own goals and time limits can drift into an open-ended activity in which we find it difficult to keep a sense of direction. Work promotes happiness by providing a time-structure, social contacts, a collective purpose, a sense of identity and regular activity. In the same way, school processes can help promote a sense of contentment.

The emphasis in any classroom should be on the goals and purpose of learning rather than on control. A strong task orientation needs to be created and moderate structure provided with limits set in non-controlling ways. The teaching style should be one that helps students understand that the world has predictable structure and that understanding that structure helps to know what to do in most situations (Feuerstein, 1980). These attitudes begin with planning time and end with summary time, both of which serve to emphasize order and predictability. If the classroom becomes too structured, however, some students will inject their own novelty through, among other things, misbehaviour.

This section looks at the key components of the first gear of authoritative teaching that provides the required level of structure, including maintaining attention, issuing commands, communicating rules and conveying status. But, first, it considers aspects of reverse gear.

Reverse gear

Teachers low in self-efficacy beliefs

Teachers who have a low sense of self-efficacy about their teaching skills, based on limiting beliefs about their abilities to manage students, tend to prefer a command and control approach and adopt a pessimistic view of student motivation. Consequently they stress control via strict rules, rely on sanctions and resort to punitive modes of discipline. High-efficacy teachers, in contrast, use more persuasive measures to support intrinsic interest and self-direction. They tend to view difficult students as teachable and their problems as surmountable with ingenuity and extra effort. Low-efficacy teachers put such problems down to low ability, student personality or attitude problems. The most effective teachers are those who are motivated to seek co-operation and give their power away as soon as possible, in contrast to those teachers who are driven by a fear of losing what little power they have. The agenda of the latter tends to be driven by the fear of the threat from the few rather than the welfare of the many. If they are also driven by 'ought' goals (Chapter 4) and struggle to achieve them, feelings of agitation will be added to fear.

Disruptive commands

Teachers can sometimes give commands in such a way that they provoke opposition rather than enlist co-operation. Commands that are expressed as criticism, such as 'why can't you do what you are told' or 'why do you never listen', are more likely to lead to opposition, particularly from boys and especially if they are given in public. If teachers are too angry when they give a command, they may shout and so inadvertently encourage opposition in retaliation to the implied criticism. Just like the body's response to pain, we all 'shut down' in response to highly personalized negative comments. Students' feelings about themselves as worthwhile need to be considered to be of equal importance as compliance.

A 'stop' command telling students what not to do, such as 'stop shouting', may end up with the students doing the very act that has been put into their mind. 'Stay in your seat' is better than 'stop running about'. With negative commands stating what the teacher does not want the students to do, students are left to decide what to do. As the number of negative commands increase, sometimes into a 'command storm', so does disruptive behaviour, especially from boys. Commands expressed in question form such as 'do you want to tidy your desk?' leave some students confused. They may not be able to work out whether they are being told to do something or given a choice.

Sometimes teachers string together a chain of commands without giving the student a chance to comply with the first command. For some students this can cause an information overload and lead to difficulties in remembering what they have to do. A similar chain command is saying the same thing repeatedly. If the teacher has the habit of repeating instructions, the students learn there is no need to comply until the last one. Such repeated commands reinforce non-compliance through the attention it gives. Commands are best stated only once.

With a 'let's' command, such as 'let's clear up this mess', if the teacher does not help, the students probably will not bother either. At the same time the teacher should not ask students to do something and then start doing it before allowing the students the chance to do it themselves.

First gear – authoritative teaching

Maintaining attention

It is important for teachers first of all to gain and maintain the attention of students, and it is mainly the teacher's non-verbal behaviour that affects the quality of this attention. If a teacher is bored, then he or she is likely to speak in a monotonous voice, use limited gestures and make little eye contact. Teachers who are insufficiently prepared for a lesson or who have worries about the class may show hesitant speech.

Facial signals such as blushing and a sweating forehead are particularly obvious to students and may be difficult for the teacher to control. Facial expressions are hard to fake. We know, for example, when someone is pretending to be pleased to see us. Forced 'air steward' smiles use a different set of muscles from a real smile. The former is under voluntary control while the latter is involuntary.

Expressions of anger also use muscles that cannot be controlled voluntarily and, so, genuine expressions of anger are hard to fake.

Variation in the tone of voice can be considerable for the tense teacher, to the extent that he or she talks in a high-pitched screech when annoyed. In contrast, teachers who are knowledgeable and interested in their subject use more gestures, eye contact and vary the tone and volume of their voice.

The gestures of good communicators illustrate the verbal message. Teachers' speech will have rhythm and emphasis; their gestures and facial expressions will have a corresponding rhythm and emphasis. The movement of their head and hands, breathing, changes in pitch, voice speed or volume, all tend to occur in combinations that are co-ordinated. In good speakers we seldom notice this non-verbal activity because its function is to draw our attention to the meaning of the message. With poor communicators the non-verbal signals can become an amusing distraction for students.

Because non-verbal signals are so powerful, students react to them even though they may not be aware of it. Sometimes it is information about the teacher's confidence that is being transmitted. It is often difficult to suppress these messages, but the first step is to be aware of them.

Authoritative commands

Co-operation-enlisting commands are more likely to be specific commands that are expressed in positive terms. Commands need to be clear rather than vague, such as 'be careful', 'be nice for a change'. The class needs to be settled and spoken to quietly rather than the teacher shouting out instructions when the class is noisy. Some will not hear what the teacher says and it will give the impression that such a noise level is acceptable. The teacher should pause and wait for the class to be quiet or remind students that all eyes need to be on the teacher before any command is given. Paraphrasing the original command avoids being seen to repeat the instruction. It is better to give signals that prepare students to attend to instructions, particularly to make transitions. 'When then' commands tell students in advance the exact consequences of their actions. For example, 'when you are sitting down, then I'll help you with your work.'

Sometimes teachers can give too many explanations, thinking that they will get more co-operation. But for some students it will be an invitation to divert the teacher from the command. Commands are best kept short and to the point. Any rationale should be brief and should either precede the command or follow compliance, and any protests should be ignored.

Communicating rules

Students thrive on the security created by familiar routines that make their lives predictable and, therefore, easier to understand. Like the lines on a football pitch, boundaries define what is in play and out of play, show where the goal is located and help assess progress. They provide clarity without necessarily limiting the ways students can choose to get their work done. Like the fence along a cliff, rules give a feeling of security that lets students explore the space right up to the edge. They should maximize space for students rather than be constricting like a cage.

Student rule-breaking can be considered as learning experiences. Boys in particular like to explore the limits of their environment. It is only by breaking a rule that students learn that the rule really means something (Rogers, 1991). Communicating rules should be more a matter of instruction than control. Once rules are successfully taught there is less need for repeated rule enforcement. The following procedures should be considered:

■ Teach rules, routines and penalties systematically in the first lessons.
■ Give model presentations of rules and routine.
■ Allow time for practice and questions.

- ▧ Provide feedback and review of rules during the first week or so.
- ▧ Check understanding of rules by means of a quiz early in the term.
- ▧ Praise students when following the rules and routines appropriately.
- ▧ Be thorough in following through on consequences.
- ▧ Plan to review procedures with the class at regular intervals.
- ▧ Apply rules, routines and penalties fairly and consistently.
- ▧ Occasionally highlight compliance with rules.

Some teachers like to discuss the need for rules and routines with students. This practice has the advantage that the rationale underlying the rules may become clearer to the students and, so, they may feel more inclined to obey the rules. However, most experienced teachers initially make most of the rules unilaterally. This approach is logical during early encounters, since a considerable number of rules would already have to exist for an orderly discussion about rules to take place! Discussion about rules is probably best postponed until the teacher has established a basic framework. Thereafter, in the higher gears, rules can be negotiated which will help teachers reach the optimal stage of student autonomy within an agreed and shared set of rules.

The nature and number of rules a teacher tries to operate is an important consideration. Vague objectives, such as 'Students must enter and leave the classroom properly', would need to be translated into more explicit and precise statements. It is important that students understand exactly what is required of them. Nevertheless, the overall emphasis should be on sensible self-control rather than on a long list of petty instructions. Too many rules can be more trouble than they are worth. Rules should be positive and expressed in terms of appropriate behaviour. They should both reflect and implement the values of the school. Rules to suppress tend to encourage what they prohibit. Rules to highlight the desired behaviours are preferable; for example, 'speak respectfully' or 'show good manners' instead of 'don't shout out'. When the child breaks a rule the teacher can explain why the behaviour fell short of the desired conduct; for example, 'I lose track of what I am saying if you shout out'.

If the rules are displayed it provides an easy reference and makes it obvious that they apply to everyone. Rules that are followed inconsistently by students, despite considerable practice and consistent application by the teacher, probably need to be reconsidered. Individuals are far less likely to misbehave in an orderly climate where the demands are explicit and realistic. Rules should be kept to the few 'unbreakable' rules. Most importantly, student motivation to comply with rules will be enhanced the more they can feel a sense of ownership of the rules.

The rules should make students accountable but accountability is different from culpability. Some teachers and students think it is a way of determining who is to blame when things go wrong, while others see it as a process for clarifying responsibility and facilitating ownership. A good accountability system should focus primarily on how to identify students who merit positive recognition.

Providing consistency

Students, and indeed adults, need consistency of rules and routines for a sense of security. People discover the value of completing a particular sequence, such as getting ready for examinations, consistently in the same order. Although this tendency may be understood as being superstitious, the benefits accrue from the order and predictability that the routine provides. We all have personal experiences of inconsistency from other people and know how it can affect us. Students have varying capacities to deal with inconsistency. A popular teacher, just like a popular celebrity with the public, is likely to be a predictable person. It is vital that individual teachers avoid unpredictability as this can cause significant student distress. Arbitrary and capricious discipline is especially damaging to student motivation because it creates a feeling of helplessness.

Fairness sometimes means treating students who do the same thing differently. The key rule is that everyone is entitled to have their personal circumstances taken into account. Consistency is a goal towards which schools will strive continuously without ever achieving it.

Conveying status

Status is no longer handed to teachers in a ready-made state. It has to be earned with each new group, largely through the teacher's personal qualities (Robertson, 1981). Like other social concepts, authority is best understood as a subjective, dynamic interaction. We expect people in authority to behave in certain ways. If strangers act as if they have authority, we tend to endow them with high status. Therefore, in wanting to establish status with new groups, the teacher has to act as if he or she had that status in the first place. Generally, high status behaviour is typified by calm assurance. Teachers showing high status tend to appear relaxed, exercise control over eye contact and share common territory.

Sometimes teachers attempt to establish their authority by a display of threat and aggression (Bugental *et al.*, 1999). This may be successful if it is used very occasionally and by a teacher who normally uses other high status behaviour. If it is used frequently, it will be seen as an attempt to maintain authority by dominating and it increases the likelihood of the teacher's authority being challenged, particularly from male students who resent being overcontrolled. High-status behaviour, therefore, is different from dominance behaviour in that it recognizes the rights and feelings of students and does not seek to degrade them. Authoritative teachers will talk to students in the same way they would talk to colleagues and will avoid comments such as 'shut it' or 'move it'. Students do not like teachers who are either too strict or not strict enough. The teacher needs to find a balance between these two extremes.

Authoritative teachers maintain status by behaving in a confident, quiet and assertive way. Raising their voice when necessary will detract nothing from their status. Teachers, who frequently shout, are overdominant or make emphatic assertive gestures, however, can give the impression of being unsure of their status. It almost implies that they expect their authority to be challenged. To maintain high status the teacher has to direct the conversation. If a student manipulates the teacher into responding to his or her questions, he or she has temporarily gained power at the expense of the teacher. If a class intimidates a teacher, he or she will not be relaxed and will begin to show low-status, tense behaviour. The students will then be controlling the teacher's actions rather than the teacher controlling their behaviour.

Body language is not just an alternative to speech, but is part of a multi-channel communication system through which to convey meaning (Bull, 2002). Through this system, parts of the body of a speaker are closely synchronized with speech, especially vocal stress. Posture can also reveal a great deal about a person's confidence and can produce a strong emotional reaction in others. A teacher can demonstrate that he or she is relaxed not only by standing, sitting or moving comfortably, but also by unhurried speech, easy use of gesture and relaxed face muscles.

Second gear – moving towards autonomy

Once established, authority is best kept to a minimum and opportunities for student initiative and autonomy maximized. Teaching today is not a matter of issuing orders and expecting blind obedience. Influencing students is more a matter of practising the skills of communicating, negotiating and mediating in a confident and authoritative manner. The development of responsibility and the teacher's orientation towards autonomy are closely linked to student motivation (Deci and Ryan, 1987). The feeling of being in control has a significant effect on student involvement in learning, particularly for boys.

Mocking and evading teacher authority is part of the universal peer culture, especially male culture, as is bending the rules a little. These activities help to preserve student autonomy and are sensibly accommodated to an appropriate extent by most teachers. Autonomy support refers to how much freedom a student is given to determine his or her own behaviour – the opposite is excessive coercion.

The equality principle has challenged the old structures of authority, and leadership is now taking on new forms. It is easy to issue commands and enforce them with punishment. It is harder to negotiate to overcome opposition and win consent. To be motivating the authority figure needs to be seen as legitimate, trustworthy, knowledgeable and likeable.

The teacher is strict for the benefit of the students not for him or herself. Indeed, classroom power should be shared as much as possible with students, with opportunities for student initiative, autonomy and control over their learning maximized. If the teacher shares some power with students, he or she will not lose power but, in fact, accrue more as the students will give the teacher more respect.

Informal situations in the classroom, and more readily in outdoor education contexts, can allow the relationship between the teacher and students to be (temporarily) made more equal. Extra-curricular activities in general appear to provide more involvement in school, especially where they offer the opportunity for meaningful participation (Masten and Coatsworth 1998). Supported study sessions also offer a different set of relationships. Breakfast and after-school clubs provide a 'border country' where the teacher's role can be renegotiated and concern for the well-being of both student and teacher can be fostered (Nixon, Walker and Barron, 2002). In recent years the students have become the teachers and the teachers the learners with the advent of information and communication technology (ICT) skills, particularly mobile telephone text messaging. Such situations offer reciprocity and 'give and take' that builds trust and encourages co-operation by allowing teachers to model compliance to the student requests. These experiences let each party know the other is human. Some teachers are not comfortable with this kind of interaction for fear of not being able to recoup their authority. When the parties revert back to normal, however, students know they are playing a role that demands a certain power relationship.

The value of humour

Displays of humour from a teacher serve a similar purpose. A teacher who can share humour with the class will be far less likely to have his or her authority challenged. Humour signals that the teacher does not take him or herself too seriously and it avoids any sense of pomposity and superiority. Laughter signals trust and a shared sense of purpose. It can be useful to soften a potentially threatening critical message. Humour also has the advantage of creating smiles and laughter that make everyone feel good. Smiles and laughter strengthen relationships, communicating that everyone is comfortable with each other. Smiling is impossible to fake and forced laughter is easy to detect.

Third gear – student empowerment

Giving students leadership roles, choices and a share of responsibilities and opportunities for decision-making will foster active participation and a sense of ownership in the learning process (Deci and Ryan, 2000). Even seemingly trivial or illusory choices have significant benefits. Teachers can provide choices where the alternatives are prearranged so that the choice will always be acceptable. Even when most of the decision-making is delegated to students, teachers need to play a 'co-investigator role' (Friere, 1970) in defining the activities and modelling the language and skills of competency.

Students need help to develop the skills that will enable them to take responsibility for their own learning. Schools are increasingly setting up opportunities to consult meaningfully with students. Students, however, need to be trained in this process from an early stage. Token or one-off efforts will not be fruitful. Participation is not necessarily the same as empowerment. Participation can involve lots of responsibility and decision-making but in relatively unimportant areas, like keeping the common room tidy, and is often on the teachers' terms. Responsibilities become real when they are on the students' terms and, for example, allow students to ask difficult questions about the school and give real feedback to teachers.

Opportunities should be created for students to identify and make decisions about their learning goals. Students will benefit from having discretion in setting schedules, work methods, when and how to check quality, when to start and stop, take breaks and prioritize and so on. Students need support to generate their own ideas about topics. Genuine student involvement is an essential part of the learning process and is encouraged through problem solving, role-playing and stimulation. Students should be asked for their views about what helps them to learn best and how teaching could be improved. Self-determined learning is encouraged through planning and self-monitoring, and cannot be nurtured in an oppressive climate. Regular negotiation with students not only emphasizes their ability to plan and choose, but also develops their capacity to take responsibility and anticipate the consequences of their actions.

9 Stimulation – Effective Teaching and Learning

Examiner: Billy – what does it feel like when you're dancing?

Billy: Don't know … sort of stiff and that at first but it sort of feels good … once I get going. I forget everything. I sort of disappear … sort of disappear … I can feel a change in my whole body, like this fire in my body … just there, I'm flying … like a bird … Like electricity … yeh … like electricity.

From the film *Billy Elliot*

This chapter describes the key aspects of the stimulation driver, including the components of task values, the process of maintaining momentum, encouraging student ownership of the learning process and the features of intrinsically motivating activities.

What is Task Value?

One of the most common notions of motivation involves values, the idea that students will only be motivated when they are interested in the activity or believe it is important to them. Components of task value include:

- *Attainment value* – The importance of doing well in a task and the extent to which it allows a student to confirm important aspects of the self.
- *Interest value* – The enjoyment students experience when doing a task.
- *Utility value* – The usefulness of the task for future goals.
- *Cost* – The negative aspects of engaging in the task, including the amount of effort required and the anticipated feelings.
- *Autonomy* – Having the autonomy to choose tasks over others is critical for the development of task values.

These components operate together to determine the value a task might have for an individual. Task values may be particularly important when making choices but not as important for performance as expectancy beliefs (Jacobs and Eccles, 2000). This implies that it may be more important to encourage self-competence beliefs to improve achievement than to worry too much about increasing students' interest in the course materials. It is unclear, however, whether students become good at something and then start to value it, or whether valuing it leads to more time spent on the task out of which competence develops.

Task value beliefs usually decline with age, with a decreased investment by students in academic activities and increased investment in non-academic activities, particularly during the middle grades of secondary education (Anderson and Maehr, 1994). It is not merely that effort is seen by some young people as progressively less important to success, but also because students' conception of intelligence may change so that needing to try hard comes to signify lesser ability. As students grow older, their beliefs about the nature of ability sometimes change from a view of ability as malleable to a view of ability as fixed. If students do poorly in certain subjects and attribute this to low ability then they may adopt a self-protective stance and lower the value of these subjects. Also as students grow older they compare themselves more with others, which can lead to lower perceptions of ability. If ability perceptions go down, then value perceptions may also decline.

Values are of limited benefit without vision. Students with a positive sense of their future do better at school and life in general. Vision affects the choices we make and how we decide to spend our time. A compelling future-orientated vision is the main force that has been found to keep people going in crisis situations (Snyder, 1994).

First gear – maintaining momentum

A motivating classroom requires organization and planning. Transitions between activities are made efficiently following a brief signal or a few directions, and the students know where they are supposed to be, what they should be doing and what equipment they need. Activities move along at a brisk pace. Just like an advanced driver, the teacher operates at maximum speed with maximum control. The classroom seems to work automatically. Well-functioning classes, however, do not just happen but result from continual efforts to create, maintain and occasionally restore conditions that foster effective learning (McLean, 1990).

The objectives are clearly stated early and lessons get off to a brisk start. Students know well in advance what they are going to do and, so, anticipate the demands of the task. When we prepare for a task we use the pre-frontal cortex, the area of the brain that moves us to action. Without any preparation the pre-frontal cortex does not activate in advance, so the more prior activation the better the performance will be.

Beginning a class with something novel arouses attention in students; a class is never started the same way day after day. The teacher speaks clearly, is always audible and avoids using language that is muddled, ambiguous or too difficult. The teacher avoids slowing down the pace of the lesson with elaborate explanations. Teaching, like any balancing act, requires momentum (Kounin, 1970). There is good organization of student movement, group composition and flow of events and equitable distribution of attention, praise and resources. The work set is appropriate to the age and abilities of the students. The lessons offer a variety of activities and teaching methods. The teacher conveys enthusiasm and interest for the topic and activities.

Students gain from having communication with the teacher. The teacher speaks to the whole class and increases the overall number of contacts with students, enabling a greater number of 'key' points to be received by all students. A balance of contacts between individuals and the whole class is more beneficial than a total emphasis on communicating with individuals or groups.

Questioning

The teacher uses appropriate questioning techniques including:

■ looking around the group(s) before calling on someone
■ keeping the students in suspense about who will be called on next by selecting randomly, while being careful not to intimidate introverted students
■ getting around to everyone frequently
■ not naming the targeted pupil until the after question to keep all pupils engaged
■ asking for volunteers to raise their hands
■ throwing out challenges by saying the next question will be difficult
■ asking students to comment on or correct a response
■ using 'how' question: 'How did you know?' 'How else could you do that?' 'How can you find out what to do next?' Such questions help to focus students' attention on their own thinking processes
■ challenging both correct and incorrect responses while accepting as much as possible of students' responses ('Yes, but … ').

Challenging a correct answer conditions the students against the expectation that a challenge by the teacher automatically means that they are wrong. A 'correct' challenge might be: 'Yes, that's right. How did you know that should be the answer?'

Getting the students to ask their own questions, to which they will usually know the answers will let students discover they know more than they think.

Girls tend to need to be certain before they will commit themselves and, so, can be more reluctant to answer questions, although they are perhaps more likely to know the answer. Boys are greater risk-takers and attention-seekers who will dominate any question and answer session. Setting prompts in advance and then pairing off boys and girls or forming gender-balanced groups can minimize this imbalance. The girls' more reflective style can modify boys' impulsivity, while the boys' confidence can encourage the girls.

Teachers are usually in a hurry and seek answers to their questions very quickly. They tend not to wait for pupils to answer a question, and elicit answers from only a small minority (Black and Williams, 2002). Consequently, a small minority of students tend to answer the majority of questions and many students are given the message that they will not be able to answer and so need not even try. The teacher can avoid this by waiting a little longer for the answer or asking students to work out the answers in groups.

Accountability

The teacher gives advance notice that he or she will be checking work and so makes the students accountable. Brief, snappy questions are used as a means of checking comprehension and keeping students 'on their toes'. The teacher makes regular spot checks of how students are working and the length of time being spent on tasks.

Students are held accountable for completing work on time and are taught to pace themselves. Time is given to review independent work so that difficulties can be identified and help given. Completed work is returned as soon as possible. Work standards appropriate to the individual student are consistently maintained.

First gear, as depicted above, is essentially a receptive-transmission model of teaching, where the teacher is the expert who provides most of the information to passive students and the content is non-negotiable (Askew, 2000).

Second gear – ownership of the learning process

Second gear entails an approach where the students construct their knowledge via participatory learning, open-ended questioning, discussion, problem-solving and discovery learning (Askew, 2000). Students are as active as possible in their own learning through projects, experiments, debates, role-play, simulation and creative applications. Students work, for example, on misspellings from their own writing by using a spelling log to help them take control of their learning while letting teachers monitor their progress. The curriculum is related to students' lives and experiences. Abstract content is made more concrete, personal and familiar.

The learning process can be emphasized by, for example, occasionally having students tear up their work at the end of the lesson, signalling the main point was the process and not the product. Similarly, answers provided at the back of the book signals that the answers are less important than the process.

Motivating attitudes, such as patience, persistence and making the most of mistakes are modelled. Teachers can show their students how they enjoy a challenge by their enthusiasm for hard tasks, by talking about how satisfying it is to work hard, by modelling looking for new and better ways to approach tasks, discussing what they have learned from their mistakes and encouraging these attitudes in the students when they are working.

A sense of progress

The teacher is well prepared and able to move at a brisk pace, and so gives students a sense of progress that builds their self-competency beliefs. There are few interruptions owing to failure to bring or prepare a prop, confusion about what to do next, the need to stop and consult the teacher's manual, false starts or backtracking to present information that should have been presented earlier. Minor fleeting inattention is ignored. More serious inattention is dealt with before it escalates into disruption, but in ways which are not disruptive themselves; for example, moving near the inattentive student, using eye contact where possible, directing a question to the student or getting his or her attention with a brief comment – 'Johnnie, I can only see you when you are in your seat'. The lesson is not interrupted unnecessarily by extended lectures or other over-reactions that would focus attention on the inattentive student rather than the lesson content.

Transitions

The teacher is sensitive to progress in deciding when to initiate transitions. Students have clear instructions at transition times, so that excessive noise or movement is avoided. Transitions are organized so that there is no 'dead time' between one activity and the next (Kounin, 1970). When students finish an activity early they have clear instructions on what to do next. The teacher avoids introducing or following up 'red herrings', stopping one activity, embarking on another, then returning to the original activity or starting one activity and then leaving it hanging.

Motivating activities

Students' perceptions of the task influence how they approach it and use their time. The tasks set give students information about their ability and will influence their willingness to learn.

Students will have optimal motivation when they have achievable, specific and short-term goals to attain, feel confident about performing well and hold realistic aspirations. For any task to be motivating, students have to see a possibility of attaining the goal. It is a great advantage if there is a fairly accurate match between the students' aspirations and their current ability level. The goal or purpose of the activity needs to be clear and considered as appropriate and legitimate, and a convincing rationale is helpful.

The more engaging the task the less students will compare how they are doing to others, performance differences will be less likely to be translated into ability differences and, so, students will be less likely to develop a performance attitude to achievement.

Encouraging a mastery attitude

The most motivating classroom encourages a mastery attitude by emphasizing an 'improve yourself' rather than a 'prove yourself' approach to learning, task mastery rather than performance and the learning process more than the product. The beliefs are conveyed that ability is not fixed, that students are competent enough to learn the material being taught. The teacher communicates how much everyone is learning, that there are many ways to succeed and that students who are less able are equally valued.

Students are encouraged to recognize their own strengths and attribute success to their knowledge, skills and effort and to put failure down to insufficient effort or inappropriate strategies rather than to a lack of ability. They are encouraged to satisfy their own interests and curiosity rather than to please the teacher, and to be independent and not rely on the teacher. They are taught how to think as opposed to what to think.

Some students can engage in negative self-talk based on previous experience and on how others respond to them. It is important to help students replace such self-defeating language with more positive self-talk, for example by having a rule that for every negative comment about themselves they need to make two positive statements. Students' perspectives and feelings should be checked and acknowledged from time to time. Ideally the teacher is more a facilitator than a subject teacher.

Third gear – intrinsic motivation

In third gear, students are helped to construct their own ways of processing knowledge and making it their own (Cooper and McIntyre, 1996) in a collaborative and reflective process, involving critical investigation and a reorganization of knowledge. The teacher encourages a dialogue between students, and the teacher–student relationship is more equal. In such an emancipating curriculum the students take control of their own learning as autonomous learners (Grundy, 1987).

We are intrinsically motivated when we want to do something for its own sake, interest and enjoyment, when we get a feeling of satisfaction during rather than after an activity (Deci, 1975). Students are adept at directing their own learning on tasks seen as interesting, fun, meaningful or relevant (McCombs, 1993). Intrinsically motivating activities have the following features (Lepper and Hodell, 1989):

- *Relevance.* Tasks are engaging to the extent that they are personally meaningful and interesting. Contextualized learning involves being able to see the value and relevance of the skills being learned as opposed to learning that is abstract and divorced from real life (Feuerstein, 1980; Haywood, 1993). Learning is best placed in meaningful contexts that show its inherent utility and capitalizes on students' interests.
- *Manageable challenge.* Motivating tasks are engaging to the degree they challenge the individual's present capacity while permitting some control. The optimal challenge is one that is set just ahead of skill level, that takes students beyond their 'comfort zone' while permitting some degree of control. Such a zone of proximal development is the space between what students can do on their own and what they can do with teacher help (Vygotsky, 1978).
- *Curiosity.* Motivating tasks have variety and diversity, and create curiosity by being surprising. Curiosity is elicited by activities that fill a gap in the student's present knowledge. Curiosity also depends on providing sufficient complexity so that outcomes are not always certain.
- *Control.* Motivating tasks foster control by allowing a sense of choice and self-determination (Deci and Ryan, 1985). Allowing students choice in activities and participation in establishing rules and procedures fosters perceptions of control. Students are not motivated to do things when they believe their actions bear little relationship to outcomes. Enjoyment of exploratory and manipulative activities also gives students a sense of control.
- *Fantasy.* Assignments are captivating to the extent that they elicit fantasy, the creation of imaginary circumstances that permit the free use of one's growing abilities. Activities that help learners become involved in make-believe, such as simulation and game-like elements, can add meaning to what might otherwise be a boring activity.

Relevance, challenge, control, curiosity and fantasy; all five of these intrinsic motivators are present in play, the starting point for formal learning. Play is the evolutionary mechanism that pulls all the intrinsic motivation strings to facilitate children's interaction with their environment. It helps them develop skills and acquire relevant information about the environment (Lepper and Henderlong, 2000). Any curriculum needs to be designed to take advantage of these basic motives.

Students should be responsible for generating interest, if they find the work boring, by seeking ways to make it more challenging and worthwhile for themselves. A combination of the above features creates activities that promote a sense of competence, accomplishment and, ultimately, positive feelings.

'Flow' – the optimal form of intrinsic motivation

The student in a state of 'flow' is completely involved in an activity, to the point of forgetting time and everything else but the activity itself (Csikszentmihalyi, 1990). 'Flow' is like a current that carries the learner along, like being on 'automatic pilot', like electricity – as Billy in the film *Billy Elliot* described how he felt when he danced. It is well illustrated by the artist engrossed in the studio, the student on an outward-bound programme (Ewert, 1989), or even the young student happy in class working on his or her sewing. The key features of flow include clear goals, a good match between the challenge and skills level, performing to the limits of one's abilities, and immediate and unambiguous feedback. It offers the most complete expression of peak performance. The challenge–skill match is displayed in Diagram 9.1. 'Flow' can be seen as the ideal way to teach students, motivating them from the inside, using their positive states to draw them into learning.

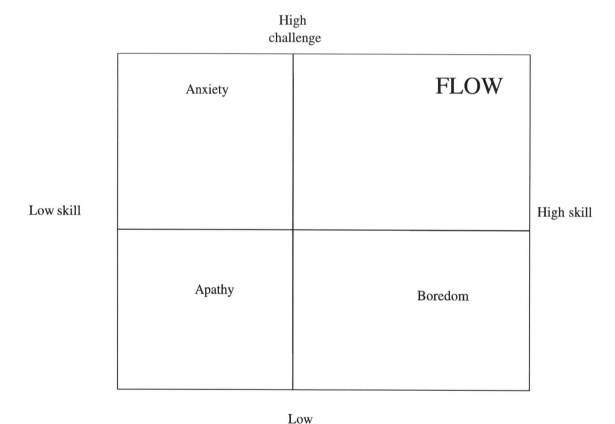

Diagram 9.1 ▓ The challenge–skill match

Thoughts, feelings and all the senses are focused on the same goal. We act with a deep but effortless involvement that takes away any worries and frustrations. The self becomes more complex as a result of flow because overcoming a challenge inevitably leaves a person feeling more capable.

One of the most common descriptions of optimal learning experiences is that time does not pass the way it ordinarily does. In general, most people report that time seems to pass much faster. But occasionally the reverse occurs. During the flow experience the sense of time bears little relation to the passage of time as measured by the clock. Students are in flow when they need to ask during a double period 'was that the first or second bell?'.

Most exceptionally high achievers will regularly experience 'flow'. For some students not constructively engaged in school, sport or leisure activities, the need for 'flow 'experiences may be met through the excitement of violence, vandalism, drugs or, even, setting off the fire alarm.

Space

One important feature of a motivating curriculum has not yet been mentioned, namely space, or periods of non-activity. This is uncommon in schools, driven by the need to get through the crowded curriculum. 'Boredom time', however, can be of significant value. It is the one chance students have to daydream and to call upon their inner resources, which are perhaps more important to a student's development in the long run than constant activity.

Reverse gear

The vagueness of much project work illustrates tasks that fail to provide any of the aforementioned features. This is particularly the case for many boys who find writing a torment and drudgery and do not see any reason for writing.

Another common example of demotivating work is when students are asked to complete numerous examples of the same task, such as changing 20 examples of fractions into decimals. Although the students may initially have been interested in the task, they can see no point in completing vast quantities of the same task. This duplication is particularly off-putting for students with specific learning difficulties who find repetitive tasks exhausting.

Narration sickness is another example, created by the teacher doing all the talking and the students all the listening (Freire, 1970). Tasks that ask students to think things out for themselves are more engaging than performance-orientated tasks that rely on surface strategies and short-term goals, like copying or rote learning (Anderson and Maehr, 1994).

Overdirected learning or what Freire termed the 'banking deposit method' reinforces students' fatalistic views of themselves in contrast to 'problem posing' education that is transforming and affirms students as being in the process of becoming (Freire, 1970).

10 Learning through Feedback

This chapter covers the general principles behind the feedback driver. It covers applications including dealing with failure, how to give critical feedback and apply punishments, reprimands, rewards and praise. It concludes with a consideration of a climate of open feedback and the nature of encouragement.

What is Feedback?

The way in which students are evaluated is perhaps the most important driver affecting the motivation mindsets. Student perception of the meaning of any evaluation is particularly important (Kamins and Dweck, 1998). Feedback has different purposes shaped, among other things, by the teacher's assumptions about learning (Askew and Lodge, 2000). The purposes of giving feedback to students are many and include:

- approving or disapproving
- controlling
- giving recognition, encouraging and affirming
- raising self-competency beliefs.

The teacher's goal may be student conformity, understanding, confidence or motivation. If the purpose is to motivate, feedback needs to provide information about what went well and the student's behaviour and skills that contributed to the success. Feedback should always be given for the benefit of the child and not to make the adult feel better. Feedback has to provide accurate, credible and relevant information about student performance. Telling students they are good at something when they have struggled to succeed will not raise their self-efficacy. Relevant feedback that provides information to judge progress, repair mistakes and redirect effort is crucial for progress towards a goal.

The feedback students receive has a direct influence on their attitudes to achievement. For example, global or ability feedback, such as 'I am disappointed/pleased with how slow/smart you are' may help encourage a performance attitude. The mother who referred to her son in front of him during a discussion with the teacher as 'a disappointment' would surely have little idea of the profound impact on her child's attitude to achievement. Students who receive such feedback may be encouraged to be self-judgemental and, in turn, respond badly to criticism. Specific strategy feedback on the other hand – 'you're working very hard' or 'You have done well to think of another way to solve the problem' – tends to encourage a mastery attitude. Students' beliefs about ability that help shape their achievement attitudes are themselves quite dynamic and can be readily influenced by the kind of feedback they are given.

Dealing with Failure

Just as gambling is about losing as much as winning, so learning involves coming to terms with failure as much as with progress. Success and failure are subjective states rather than objective realities. Response to setbacks is like a fork in the road, leading to either continued effort or giving up (Thompson, 1999). It is also a watershed in that success and failure do not shade gradually into one another. Rather, persistence often gives way abruptly to giving up.

Feelings of deteriorating skills can be particularly demotivating. This explains why some people suddenly stop participating in activities such as sports despite their relatively high skill level.

Students' experiences of how teachers deal with their failures are crucial in shaping their lifelong attitudes to learning. Adult recollections of defining moments that shaped their attitudes to learning invariably relate to how teachers communicated critical feedback or handled their failure.

Failure can have a bigger and longer-lasting impact than success. It triggers the stress hormone cortisol that makes us feel anxious, frightened and exhausted. Failure produces a slower heart rate. Blood flows out of the gut to give that 'sinking feeling', our muscles slacken and we lose control of our limbs. The neurotransmitters immobilize and so protect the brain. This chemical reaction is designed to make sure we do not make the same mistake again (Winston, 2002).

Explanations for failure can be 'progress orientated' and keep the door open to progress or 'failure-accepting' and close the door to progress (Clifford, 1984). We cannot and should not insulate students from failure. It helps determine the value of success. Failure also plays an important part in building self-efficacy. It is better, therefore, to develop a tolerance of failure by encouraging ways of dealing with it. A skilful combination of success and failure is better for stimulating achievement than a 'neutral' atmosphere. Failure can be used to motivate already successful students.

While accurate feedback about the reasons for failure is always better than 'false' feedback designed to maintain student self-esteem, it needs to be given sensitively and to link failures with its causes, particularly with controllable factors such as low effort and inappropriate strategies. In this way it will shape optimistic attributions and offer encouraging information on self-efficacy. Teacher criticism is a more potent weapon than many realize and is one of the most common threats to student self-competency. Confidence, like a house, is quicker to demolish than to build.

While excessive criticism is off-putting, moderate criticism can be motivating when it conveys a belief that students can do better with more effort. It can inform students of the value of lessons and provides benchmarks in progress towards goals. It is best used judiciously and balanced with positive feedback in situations where other approaches have been tried.

How teachers respond to wrong answers sends strong messages to students about the nature of mistakes and their role in learning. Teachers need to treat mistakes in a way that encourages students to see them as helpful opportunities for learning. Correcting mistakes quickly does not do much to facilitate learning. Mistakes are a necessary part of learning and also offer information about how a student learns. They do not necessarily reflect sloppiness, laziness or inadequacy.

The level of anxiety experienced as a result of failure should be monitored and components of the curriculum leading to failure reduced or replaced for discouraged students. Students need help in discovering their capabilities and setting realistic goals for themselves. Repeated failure does not help them to make a reasonable estimate of their capabilities.

Factors shaping how students respond to failure

Managing students' failure will be informed by an understanding of their motivation mindsets and self-esteem, which shape how they make sense of and deal with failure.

Failure for students with a fixed idea about ability is likely to be seen as a measure of their fixed intelligence and so can trigger a poor response. To students with an incremental idea of ability it probably means they have not worked out how to do the task properly or they need to try harder.

Students with a mastery attitude see difficulties as a challenge and cope well with mistakes. Such students treat failure as a signal that they need to try harder or do something differently. Learners with a performance attitude, on the other hand, tend to react self-critically to mistakes and come to believe in the inevitability of failure

Some students motivated by a fear of failure blame their lack of ability for failure but take little credit for success. The sub-group with 'learned helplessness' overassimilate negative feedback into their view of themselves as hopeless and may see offers of help as confirming their lack of competence. Repeated attribution of failure to stable, internal, uncontrollable and global factors suggests failure is inevitable.

The helpless response is based on the view that failure is out of one's control and it rapidly leads to self-blame, less persistence and a worsening performance (Diene and Dweck, 1980). Trying to change the rules, becoming distracted or giving up are symptoms of the helpless attitude. Any sense of strategy can get lost, resulting in wild guessing. Helpless students can see difficulties as so insurmountable they cannot get themselves organized to sort things out even when very little is needed. Negative self-talk is common. Such despairing reactions are more likely if failure is seen as a measure of one's whole self-esteem (Thompson, 1999). Consequently, too much time can be spent worrying rather than concentrating on the task.

Another sub-group, those students with a strong performance attitude plus low competency beliefs, are particularly vulnerable to a spiral of failure avoidance to protect their self-worth. Self-worth protection, such as finding excuses or self-handicapping by not working hard (Thompson, 1999) dominate such students when failure is anticipated that will be put down to important aspects of the self, especially low ability, and when there are no excuses to let the self 'off the hook'.

Students with negative self-esteem have particular difficulties coping with failure. They cannot dismiss or ignore criticism, as they assume it is probably correct. Those with true self-esteem will be less put off by failure than those with fragile esteem who are threatened by failure. Any critical feedback for such students needs to be balanced with reminders of positive aspects and reassurances that the problems can be remedied. It is crucial to distinguish disapproval of their work from them as a person. In contrast, students with high esteem need to be criticized in ways which counter their capacity to discount deficiencies which they do not see as important and in ways which stress that the criticism is justified.

Reverse gear – damaging feedback

Unhelpful or 'killer' feedback (Askew and Lodge, 2000) destroys students' self-motivation when it is excessive and overcritical, disconnected with students' thinking and offers no scope for any dialogue or suggestions for improvement. Such feedback is driven too much by the teacher's own agenda.

Damaging critical feedback

▨ *Public comparison.* Negative feedback is most likely to damage motivation where there is public evaluation of work, severe grading standards or an emphasis on competition, or where the outcome is stressed more than the learning process. A product orientation can encourage a performance attitude where correctness, absence of mistakes and normative success are emphasized.

▨ *Disconnected.* Feedback has a crucial role in shaping students' attributions for failure. Disconnected feedback is feedback that is not under students' control (Berglas, 1985) because it is not dependent on their performances. It is dependent, instead, on such things as students' ascribed characteristics and status (for example, being a pest or the teacher's favourite), or on criteria established by the teacher but unknown to the students. It can depend on the teacher's mood. It includes feedback that is false or inappropriate for the performance. Similarly, blunt feedback without much detail of specific aspects of performance tells the student he or she has gone wrong but does not provide any clues as to how he or she can improve. Normative grading gives a rank order position but nothing else. Another form of disconnected feedback puts down success to irrelevant qualities such as good looks or a nice personality. Each type of disconnected feedback fails to let students make useful attributions and so does not help them develop any sense of self-efficacy. It does not let the student know what he or she has done or needs to do to be successful and leaves him or her uncertain.

▨ *Vague.* Even if teachers do not deliver critical feedback in words, disapproval can be expressed with a frown, a sigh or a look and so on. Or they may simply avoid contact. The student knows the teacher disapproves but does not know why or what to do about it. So, feedback needs to be clear and expressed fully. No feedback is often assumed to be bad feedback (Butler and Nisan, 1986).

▨ *Emotionally loaded.* Emotionally loaded feedback, the stuff that makes it impossible for married couples to teach each other to, for example, drive, uses terms like 'always' or 'never'. Terms that produce emotional reactions and raised defences should be avoided. Tentative words like 'sometimes' and 'perhaps' are preferable. It is best to keep to a single clear issue. The most concrete and recent example should be the focus. If rising defences are met they should be dealt with on the spot. Piling on more evidence to strengthen the case only makes the situation worse.

▨ *Judgemental/personalized.* Judgemental criticism that reflects on the child's traits or on the child as a whole (for example, 'you are a selfish child') carries an implicit threat of rejection and fosters a helpless reaction to setbacks. Reactions include self-blame and feelings of incompetence. Students can accept descriptions of their behaviour but find comments about their individual qualities threatening. For example, 'come on, you're just messing about' is easier to accept than 'you're such a pest'.

Indirect critical feedback

Although very few teachers would intentionally tell their students that they were low in ability, this information may unwittingly be conveyed, particularly when the teacher tries to protect the self-esteem of the failing student. There are four common and seemingly positive ways teachers can inadvertently give low ability cues:

▨ *Pity following failure.* Of all the subtle messages about competence in classrooms, the emotional reactions of teachers may be among the most important. If the teacher reacts angrily it suggests that controllable factors are causing the failure, inferring that the student is responsible and free to try hard or not. On the other hand pity suggests failure is down to low ability and is unavoidable, and so the student is not responsible for the failure. Pity instigates the desire to help, whereas anger triggers disapproval and the withholding of help. An empathic response avoids giving either of these emotional cues to students.

▨ *Praise for easy success.* Praise may enhance efficacy when it is tied to students' achievements. When given regardless of performance, however, it may convey low expectations and, so, can damage self-efficacy. When students believe a task is easy, praise combined with effort information ('that's good, you've been working hard') signals low ability and leaves students feeling the teacher either does not know them or rate them highly. Praise and the absence of blame leads to low-ability attributions, while criticism for the quality of work suggests high expectations.

Flattery maybe gets us anywhere with colleagues. It works because they realize it is just a game, like flirting, and they enjoy the playful element. It would not work with students who can detect plastic praise that just looks like the real thing. Students' emotional radars will detect falseness that leads to distrust.

■ *Unsolicited offers of help.* Being given help can imply to sensitive students that the cause of their difficulties is due to uncontrollable factors like low ability, while being left to get on with it suggests they are due to controllable factors such as insufficient effort (Graham and Barker, 1990). This explains why some students will sometimes destroy their work if the teacher helps them. Teachers can jump in too soon with an answer (Brophy and McCaslin, 1992). It is important to distinguish between 'instrumental help' such as probing, from 'gratuitous help' such as supplying answers outright.

■ *Easy work.* There is a temptation to give easy work to some students so that they can complete it and get a sense of achievement. This has to be used carefully as it may unwittingly reinforce feelings of helplessness. The teacher's role is not to give success to students but to put success within their grasp.

Praise erosion

The benefits of praise can be eroded in various ways; for example, when the frustrated teacher communicates that the good performance is not always forthcoming, with the common 'ah but' response, such as asking the child, 'but why can't you do that all the time?'

Contaminated praise from qualifiers such as 'but' and 'why' can twist praise into criticism. Giving praise sarcastically is another way of negating praise as in such comments as, 'Don't tell me you're actually being nice to your neighbour!' or telling the truant, 'good of you to drop in'. This negates praise, particularly for insecure students who are more likely to 'tune into' the negative comment and take it to heart. Another common form of contaminated praise is grudged praise, for example when the teacher admits to the student 'apparently you seem to have impressed some of your teachers'.

First gear – constructive criticism

In first gear the teacher controls all the feedback and gives information to passive learners. In this gear, feedback is a 'gift' (Askew and Lodge, 2000) from teachers in a one-way communication system. It is usually evaluative, pointing to the gap between student performance and the teachers' desired outcome. Progress is evaluated exclusively by the teacher. This form of feedback is most useful when the standard is explicit and the information about progress towards the standard is as clear and as concrete as possible.

Critical feedback should always start from, and build on, the student's strengths and what he or she is doing right. The student should be helped to keep the feedback in perspective by including positive comments about overall performance and by acknowledging the difficulty of the situation. Ideally, critical feedback should be sensitive and planned with consideration given to the following issues:

■ What are the most important points?
■ What is the best way to get them across?
■ What is the right amount of feedback?
■ How can it be broken into manageable bits?
■ What is the best evidence to describe what is meant?
■ What would make it balanced?
■ Should it be private or public?

To suggest that teachers should avoid criticism or give praise more freely overlooks the power of the context in determining the meaning of any message. Sympathy, lots of praise, minimal criticism and helping behaviour are useful strategies that can soften the blow of failure. But unsolicited help, pity, excessive praise and easy work can be disempowering by suggesting low ability, while moderate anger, criticism and relative neglect used judiciously and balanced with positive feedback may point out the need for more effort. A carefully chosen criticism can be motivating when it conveys a belief that students can do better with more effort and informs students of the value of lessons. Indiscriminate praise can be meaningless, and insincere praise can be detrimental to some students.

Punishment

Punishment usually has one or more of the following goals:

▓ *Deterrence.* Punishment aims to discourage students from similar misbehaviour in the future.
▓ *Rehabilitation.* Punishment aims to help students understand that their behaviour is unacceptable.
▓ *Retribution.* Justice requires that inappropriate acts are followed by deserved punishment, which meets our need for revenge.

There is often uncertainty over the role of punishment within school policies. It can certainly make teachers feel better, but there is little evidence that it does much else. At best it signals that certain behaviours are unacceptable. At worst it can be a time-consuming way of making badly behaved students worse, particularly boys. Punishment is often a short-term palliative with little long lasting effect. The possibility of detection is a far greater deterrent than any punishment.

The main value of punishment may be in meeting our emotional needs for revenge. Teachers can experience indiscipline as a threat to their pride, and the public context makes any personal slight hard to ignore. Being humiliated and feeling their self-esteem is being attacked creates a strong desire for revenge, to get even for their loss and to stop other students copying unwanted behaviour. The whole point of revenge is to make the person suffer, not the most appropriate basis to get the best out of students.

Ineffective use of punishment will either have no effect or, in some instances, may actually encourage the student to misbehave again. Punishments are sometimes like complaints in that they make you feel better but do not often lead to change. The negative side-effects can include:

▓ resentment, rebellion and retreat
▓ modelling an angry reaction to conflict and aspects of bullying
▓ failure to teach students what we want them to do, ask anything of students, encourage self-examination or change the students' ideas or feelings
▓ making students pay for mistakes
▓ focusing on the past
▓ stressing external controls
▓ affecting, like pest control, the good as well as the bad.

Public interest in bullying has acted as a catalyst to look at the culture of schools (McLean, 1996). The problem of how to deal with bullying presents a great challenge for schools, as the traditional punitive response to misbehaviour is not appropriate. Students learn more from what adults do than from what they say. Punishment can reinforce the idea that power is what matters, that force is an acceptable 'quick fix'. Imposing teacher authority comes close to aspects of bullying behaviour, namely, the intentional (ab)use of power against a person's will to cause hurt. There is a fine line between a teacher's use and abuse of power over students. Punishment says to the bully, 'you used your power over a student to hurt him and I am going to use my power to punish (hurt) you'. Indeed, some would argue this model of teacher–student interaction has contributed to a bullying culture in some schools. It builds resentment in the bullies and leads to an escalation of the bullying, with the result that students do not readily report it.

Some teachers occasionally use punishment to emphasize their authority, without due warning. While some incidents should be punished immediately, it is usually wiser and more effective to use punishment sparingly. An emphasis on punishment is likely to undermine the quality of the student–teacher relationship. Sometimes teachers construe disruption automatically as a threat to their authority and react with a controlling intervention, when in fact the problem relates to a conflict between students. Conflict mediation would perhaps be a more appropriate teaching strategy than punishment in such situations.

Effective punishments

Outlined below are guidelines for the use of punishments:

▨ Punishment is best *combined with positive strategies*. To help students do better in future we do not first need to make them feel worse about themselves.

▨ The type and severity of the punishment should fit the misbehaviour. A punishment is most *appropriate when fair* and it follows reasonably from the behaviour, so that the student can see the connection between his or her action and the consequences. Punishment should not damage any interest that helps maintain the student's motivation. Equally it is not helpful to identify learning tasks with punishments or to withdraw a child from the curriculum.

▨ Punishment is most effective when it follows *as soon as possible* after the misbehaviour. There is then a direct link between the inappropriate action and the unpleasant consequence. This is not to say that deferred punishments are ineffective. The anticipation of the punishment can have some immediate effect upon the student.

▨ If a teacher is to be seen to be fair, he or she must *consistently* punish rule infringements. Lack of consistency leads to unpredictability that is stressful for students and, in turn, leads to testing out behaviour. Sanctions, however, need to take into account individual circumstances.

▨ *The certainty is more important than the severity.* As the power of any consequence comes mainly from its certainty, the effectiveness does not depend on the scale. Consequently, breaking them into smaller bits can increase the number of punishments. For example, go to the end of the queue can become lose ten places in the queue, five places, two etc.

▨ The punishment must be *aversive* and so avoid encouraging misbehaviour. In some circumstances the punishment might act as a reward and inadvertently encourage the misbehaviour. Removal from class or exclusion from school may give disaffected students a welcome relief from tasks or add to their status among peers.

▨ Punishment does not need to be in public. Sanctions should be discrete and provide opportunities to make a *low-key response* to misbehaviour rather than be in front of the whole class.

Reprimands

A reprimand embodies a warning aimed at stopping off-task behaviour and avoiding the need for punishment. The following qualities increase the likelihood that a reprimand will be effective:

▨ Reprimands are only effective if they are *used sparingly*. Repeated use is likely to be regarded as nagging.

▨ Reprimands should have a sharp and specific *behaviour focus* rather than entail a long list of faults. The reprimand should stress disapproval of the act rather than the student.

▓ Reprimands should be *correctly targeted* at the student responsible for the misbehaviour. Individual students should be named. Blanket reprimands of the whole class annoy other students.

▓ The problem should be *defined in terms of the effect on the teacher* rather than focused on the student; for example, 'when this happens I feel angry because it keeps everyone back'. Such 'I messages' communicate how the teacher feels and what the teacher wants. 'You' messages tend to blame; for example, 'Your carrying on always keeps everyone back'.

▓ The message should explicitly and precisely *state the rule* that has been broken.

▓ A reprimand should be clear, firm and *given confidently* avoiding any suggestion of pleading for co-operation. It must be given calmly, the teacher pausing beforehand to collect his or her thoughts.

▓ The teacher must treat the student with *respect* and politeness in order for his or her disapproval to matter.

▓ The reprimand should be *solution focused* and ask what the child should be doing not why he or she is doing it. Reprimands should include how the child can do better in the future.

▓ *Quiet and private* reprimands in silence with the student's full attention are more effective than loud, public interventions, as this will give less motivation to challenge the teacher.

Praise

As more and more teachers begin to embrace the praise culture, seduced by its inherent goodness and deceptive simplicity, a deeper analysis of praise may be beneficial. Giving praise is actually a more complex and subtle process than it seems at first sight, particularly in the emotional minefield of the classroom. To use praise effectively teachers need to check out how students respond to it, particularly how they make sense of it and use it to explain their progress (Brophy, 1981).

Although most teachers acknowledge the need for and benefits of praise, they do not actually praise as often as they think (Brophy, 1981; Merret and Wheldall, 1990). Overall they give as much disapproval as approval. Academic behaviour is more likely to be praised than social behaviour that attracts more disapproval. Satisfactory behaviour is usually taken for granted and therefore passes without comment. Although most schools aspire to a praise culture, in practice praise in classrooms has been found to be non-contingent and general rather than specific. It is often dependent more on the teacher's views of the student's need for esteem-boosting rather than actual behaviour or performance.

Praise tends to lose some of its power, as students grow older. Older students may interpret praise as condescending and suggestive of low expectations. In general, it seems to be most effective with younger or less mature students, or those who still wish to please their teachers. With older students it is best couched in language that conveys information about competency and is perceived as sincere and justified.

Praise, derived from the Latin for price, is a form of valuing. It originally meant an expression of material worth. There is a fine line between controlling and affirming praise, and it is not easy to give the latter (Kamins and Dweck, 2000). Praise can be quickly rebuffed as patronizing, inaccurate or grudging. Controlling praise may lead to praise-dependent conformity (Hanko, 1993).

If the teacher is going through the motions, praise will come across as hackneyed and lacking spontaneity. Credibility and sincerity are a must or praise can be as offensive as empty compliments or ill-considered gifts, each of which signifies that the person is not really known or valued. Private forms of praise have the advantage that their value is not derived at the expense of others. Excessive praise obliges the student to live up to the high expectations it suggests or it may pressurize students to perform even better next time. Praise should focus on the task at hand, rather than link performance to future success.

Some students cannot cope with praise, as it threatens their view of themselves as unworthy. Students with low self-esteem prefer negative feedback that confirms their self-views (Swann, Pelham and Krull, 1989). Good outcomes can even damage the health of those with low self-esteem (Brown and McGill, 1989). Having concluded that you are worthless, evidence to the contrary is distressing and difficult to manage. Even a negative identity is less distressing than one that is in danger of fragmenting. With these students it may be better to be oblique and say, for example, 'That was fine but maybe you could do even better'. It is more appropriate to ask such students what they think of their performance and then comment on their evaluation rather than rush in with enthusiastic praise only to get annoyed when it is rebuffed.

Using praise effectively

Outlined below are guidelines for the use of praise:

▓ *Accuracy and honesty* are essential or praise can degenerate into empty compliments.
▓ The impact of praise can be *heightened* by smiling, warmth in the eyes, a pat on the back.
▓ *Private* forms of praise have the advantage that their value is not derived at the expense of others.
▓ With older students praise is better couched in language which conveys *information about competency* and is perceived as justified.
▓ Praise should concentrate on student efforts and effective strategies, on the *process* of their work rather than the end product or their ability.
▓ Praise should be *specific and explicit* so that the child knows why he or she is being praised. General comments like 'good' and 'well done' are less effective.
▓ *Indirect praise*, obliquely given or quiet private praise will work well with boys.
▓ A *little praise regularly* is better than a binge. Small and frequent praise is better than extravagant infrequent praise.
▓ It is best to *avoid qualifiers* such as 'but' and 'why'.

Rewards

Most students are motivated by intrinsic rewards like satisfaction and feelings of achievement. For others, the main incentive is extrinsic like examination results or public recognition. When students are not intrinsically interested in school or in getting the extrinsic rewards school offers, artificial rewards such as sweets or points are a necessary starting point. Such rewards however may damage intrinsic motivation (Cameron and Pierce, 1994; 1996; Lepper and Henderlong, 1996).

If a student is working well at something intrinsically interesting and receives a reward for good performance, he or she may attach more significance to the reward than the interest. Harnessing intrinsic interest may get harder if 'fringe benefits' such as rewards tangential to the completed work get in the way. While rewards have long been a part of school life we now have a greater than ever rewards technology and some argue that this has squeezed out both traditional school values and natural consequences. Rewards are like fireworks and thrill rides in that they need constantly to be enhanced to make an impact.

Students want to be competent and self-determining. When they think rewards are controlling their behaviour they may lose this sense of self-determination (Boggiano, Main and Katz, 1988; Ryan and Deci, 2000). In schools today the teacher is usually the one who sets the criteria for the reward. When rewards smack of surveillance, comparison with others or imply manipulation, even if thought to be for the students' own good, they may cause resentment. Student perceptions may shift from seeing their behaviour as self-initiated to reward driven. Students might then learn to do the minimum to get the reward. Once the reward is no longer available, there is nothing compelling them to work so their interest may drop. Reinforcement may initially increase the activity's frequency but when it is withdrawn students may engage in the activity even less than they did before it was introduced. So, extrinsic rewards may lead to a decrease in intrinsic motivation particularly when there is initial interest in an activity.

Offering tangible rewards as inducements to learn may cause students to select easier tasks (Pittman, Boggiano and Ruble, 1983). Students who adopt an extrinsic mentality can take on many of the characteristics associated with learned helplessness. It is important, therefore, that students who are placed on behaviour monitoring programmes with rewards are not retained on the programme for any longer than is necessary (Lepper, 1981). Despite or perhaps because of this unstable source of rewards, externally orientated students become more dependent on teacher opinion. When students are offered unnecessary rewards, they may become expedient and try to maximize rewards for minimum effort. Learning or behaving appropriately becomes the way to obtain a reward, not to satisfy curiosity or discover something of interest. Thus, students on monitoring programmes can become objectionable if the teacher does not give them the top award for minimum efforts.

Using rewards effectively

The critical element is not whether incentives are used but how they are used. A reward is defined as something that follows behaviour and causes it to happen more often. Every teacher has some form of reward system that tells students what they have to do succeed (Covington, 1998). The impact of rewards will in part be shaped by the teacher's style of engagement, particularly whether it is controlling or supportive of student autonomy. If it is controlling, the rewards will be experienced as controlling.

Principles include:

▓ Everyone should be treated in a fair and equal way. By tying rewards to specific, well-defined actions they should be *open to all*.

▓ *Real achievements* or contributions to the common good, not self-seeking gains, should be recognized. Feedback should reflect the school's core values and serve as a guide to others.

▓ Rewards *should not be emphasized beforehand* and distract attention from the activity itself. Rewards that are introduced after task completion and are unexpected are less likely to be experienced as controlling.

▓ Verbal rewards by their nature are more likely to be *informative* than tangible rewards that are more likely to be experienced as controlling.

▓ Rewards are most effective when they are sincere and form a *natural part of a student–teacher relationship.*

▓ Rewards must reflect the level of achievement being reinforced. Students must feel that the rewards are *credible* and earned.

▓ Rewards should be *withdrawn as soon as possible.*

▓ Rewards should *not be distributed on a competitive basis.*

▓ The effectiveness of any reward does not depend on how big it is. *The certainty is more important than the scale.* By breaking rewards into smaller bits the number available can be increased.

▓ Subject-orientated and rule-related rewards specify efforts and improvement, and so encourage students by *making them feel responsible for success.*

▓ One of the best ways to promote learning is to provide *rewards for increased effort.*

▓ Rewards *should never be taken away* once earned.

- Any incentives must *take student interests and aptitudes into account.*
- Rewards should be *applied as soon as possible.* Deferred rewards, however, can work with older, more mature students who are able to work towards a more distant goal.
- Rewarding *the group* can help encourage positive peer pressure.
- Rewards *should not devalue learning,* such as being let out of school early.
- *Learning activities* can be good rewards.

Second gear – formative feedback

Feedback is a way of inviting students to reflect upon their performance and see for themselves what needs to be done. Quality feedback is neutral, as if holding up a mirror so students can see themselves more clearly, particularly their new skills and capabilities. It provides an action replay of what the students did and discusses how they might do it better. Feedback is best when it has a formative effect on learning, that is, when it further develops learning (Sadler, 1989).

Feedback is most useful when it shares the teacher perspective in a way that describes rather than judges. It should invite a response from students and so help them reflect. Students should be invited to suggest ways to improve, encouraged to take the initiative and provide their own feedback.

As much information as possible should come from the students. They should be encouraged to seek information via a range of cues from themselves, peers and teachers. Students should be tutored to rate their own progress towards goals, using, for example, portfolios, and helped to exercise independent judgement. Learners should be trained to apply their own criteria for success and failure. They could be asked to express what they have learned, what contributed to their success or failure and how their new knowledge and insights would affect them.

Formative feedback emphasizes individual improvement developed through effort and specific strategies, thus helping students make optimistic interpretations of progress and so feel responsible for success. Evaluation criteria are most helpful when they are clear and allow for assessment of individual improvement rather than normative comparisons.

Immediate feedback should be given wherever possible using, for example, self-correcting materials, answer keys and by organizing students to give feedback to each other. An overemphasis on testing, however, can be demotivating if it communicates that the purpose of schooling is to succeed on the tests and that test results indicate their global ability or worth. This can be avoided if tests are seen as checking students' current skill level and effort in order to point out what they need to work on. Teachers can involve pupils in setting test questions, creating mark schemes and marking each others' answers to give pupils a more formative perspective of tests. Such approaches stress the need to understand rather than to succeed, and the tests are just assessments that point to areas that need more attention (Black and Williams, 2002).

Restorative approaches

Blame is a major barrier to change and no one responds well to being pushed into a 'fault swamp'. It is more effective to translate blame labels such as 'troublemaker' and 'pest' into actions that hold the student accountable rather than culpable, request a change in behaviour and require the student to rectify the situation. The 'no blame' approach to dealing with bullying is a good example of this principle in practice (Maines and Robinson, 1992; Pikas, 1989).

Students who are made to feel bad about themselves are less likely to be able to repair the behaviour than those who think they have done a bad thing (Tangney, 1995). They prefer to avoid the situation altogether or become angry at the person they hurt to escape their self-contempt.

Restorative approaches recognize two kinds of shame (Braithwaite, 1989; 2001). One is stigmatizing shame, which excludes and condemns the offender. By labelling the misbehaving student as someone who cannot be trusted, it tells the offender he or she is expected to continue to cause problems. The alternative is inclusive shame that condemns the misbehaviour but not the individual, and so gives the offender the opportunity to rejoin their community. To earn the right to a fresh start, offenders are invited to express remorse and repair the harm they have caused. Focusing on the misbehaviour is more effective as it involves linking the act with the punishment without emphasizing the student's personal qualities. It minimizes the risk of resentment or retaliation and avoids labelling the student. It also teaches the student to face up to the consequences of his or her behaviour but does not diminish him or her as a person.

Punishment without learning offers only authoritarian control. More sophisticated methods of making students responsible for their behaviour are needed. The aim of any strategy should be to resolve the problem rather than establish blame and guilt. Recent thinking has moved away from punishment to notions of logical consequences and solution-building (Rhodes and Ajmal, 1995). The key principles of solution-building include a search for educational solutions not problems, an allocation of responsibility not blame, looking forwards not backwards, all to resolve the problem not establish guilt.

A consequence is the result of a choice the student has made. Consequences are most appropriate when they are related to the misbehaviour, respectful of the child and revealed in advance. Having the student use a sheet of paper in class and then transfer it to his or her jotter at home might follow the student failing to bring the jotter to class. Logical consequences aim to encourage recovery by recognizing the misbehaviour as a mistake and looking for some kind of reconciliation. They are about bad choices and behaviour not bad students. Consequences allow choice and control is retained by the students.

The restorative approach recognizes that misbehaviour can be followed by the threat that everyone emerges from it further disrupted or the opportunity that injustice is recognized, equity restored and the future clarified so that participants are more respectful. It sees the situation as an opportunity for the child to learn new ways of behaving. This type of approach requires as early a response as possible, and maximum co-operation coupled with minimum coercion since repairing relationships and nurturing learning is best done within a voluntary context.

Praising effort rather than ability

Praising students for being clever has been widely assumed to be helpful in building up their confidence. Such well-meaning praise, however, can be damaging when it is seen as insincere or when it leads students to feel pressurized to produce good performances.

Praise directly communicates the attributions teachers make about students' progress. Ability praise can suggest that success is due to a quality students have rather than something they have done. It may lead students to concentrate on showing their ability rather than on learning (Mueller and Dweck, 1996). They may come to see ability as something that can be measured as well as something they cannot change. It can backfire by making students equate success with high ability but also failure with low ability. It can make students vulnerable to seeing difficulties as caused by low ability which leads to giving up in the face of setbacks. Ability praise has been found to be given to girls more than boys (Dweck *et al.*, 1978).

Praising ability puts too much focus on ability and may make students less interested in anything that challenges their ability. They overidentify with their success and then feel humiliated by failure. In a similar way, praising young people for their good looks will boost their confidence but may make them pay too much attention to how they look and become anxious if such compliments are not forthcoming.

Most teachers and parents assume it is a good idea to praise students for doing well, even on easy tasks (Mueller and Dweck, 1996). We assume praise will give students the confidence they need to succeed. Praising ability, however, is like giving out cheap credit that can build up financial problems for the future. Confidence in ability is only useful as long as students are doing well. Person praise misses the opportunity of commenting on the real accomplishment. Praising students' personal qualities may carry the same message as judgemental criticism: that you can be judged from your performance. So if students perform poorly, they turn the previous positive judgement into a negative view (Dweck, 2000).

It is more important to be confident in your capacity to deal with difficulties and to know that you will progress if you apply yourself and use the right approaches, especially when the going gets tough (Hong, Chiu and Dweck, 1995). This is more likely to result from praise for effort that encourages students to concentrate on learning as opposed to showing off their ability. Effort praise also encourages students to put their performance down to effort that is clearly under their control (Boggiano *et al.*, 1987). It emphasizes the possibility of improvement and the malleability of ability. Students who are praised for effort will be more likely to think failure means they need to try harder. This issue exemplifies how feedback allows teachers to 'drill down' to impact on students' motivation mindsets.

It is unfortunate that so many schools give effort awards as the 'booby' prize and so undermine the value of effort. When students succeed, attention should be concentrated on giving information about their efforts and effective strategies, on the process of their work, how they focused on the task and how they persisted, rather than the end product or their ability. Effective feedback does not stop at saying 'well done' but goes on to tell the student why he or she is being praised. The teacher for example says, 'Good! ... You made a plan, so now you know what to do as you go along'. Praise is only as good as the quality of information it imparts. Telling a student that he or she is 'working like a Trojan' is only motivating if the student knows what a Trojan is! As with criticism, it is better to separate the deed from the doer by praising their work habits, which communicate the value placed on their work rather than personal traits that may embarrass and be resented.

Third gear – a climate of open feedback

A motivating climate is one that makes exchanging feedback an integral part of classroom life and encourages students to seek feedback from the teacher and each other. Pupils are encouraged to mark each others' work, to think about the aim of the work and to understand the criteria of quality (Black and Williams, 2002). Feedback becomes more of a dialogue (Askew and Lodge, 2000), a reciprocal flow of influence (Senge, 1994). It is less concerned with judgement and more with maximizing learning. The role of teacher and learner are routinely exchanged. To create such a climate, teachers need to look for and be open to feedback from students to help improve their teaching. It should be made clear that feedback is welcomed by asking questions such as:

▓ What is it like being in this class?
▓ If you could change one thing about it what would it be?
▓ What can the teacher do to improve the teaching?

When given feedback the teacher should take it neutrally, ask for specific examples and suggestions for improvement, summarize what has been said to check understanding and thank the student for the feedback.

A climate of positive feedback can be encouraged through the use of compliments circles where students are invited to give each other compliments for special achievements. A weekly challenge could be set for students, such as, identify a particularly good piece of writing and say what makes it good. Students need such starting points to develop their own evaluation skills.

Encouragement

There is a significant difference between praise that gives approval to achieve conformity and encouragement that recognizes the student's efforts. The former type of praise is a reward that students can earn, with the reward of being valued by their teachers. Too much controlling praise can teach students they have to please adults to be approved. Some teachers praise students only if they do something they regard as worthwhile. Such judgemental praise is given at the end of an activity while encouragement can be given any time.

Encouragement (based on the Latin *cor* for heart or courage) is aimed at putting the heart back into students' learning by nurturing their self-belief in contrast to praise that seeks to give approval (Hanko, 1993). Performance does not have to be perfect to deserve encouragement. When students are learning a new skill they need to be reinforced for each small step. They do not need to earn encouragement. It can be given for nothing, something special, for effort or improvement, when the student is doing well or even making mistakes. Teachers encourage students when they appreciate and have faith in them and notice their efforts and feelings.

Encouragement is affirming in that it helps students feel valued just for being themselves. With encouragement students learn to appreciate their special qualities and to feel capable. This kind of interest in a student's work is more appreciative than complimenting a trait. It not only rewards students for their work but teaches them values and gives them confidence that will serve them well in the future (Snyder, 1994).

Teaching students to recognize their own achievements is important in helping them self-approve. For example, 'you must feel pleased with your project' nurtures the student's own positive recognition of his or her work. When asking the class a question and many students volunteer the answer, the teacher can ask only one student but can invite all those with the right answer to pat themselves on the back.

The main different types of praise are summarized in Diagram 10.1. They parallel the four gears of the affirmation dimension.

Gear	*Type of praise*	*Purpose*	*Goal*
Reverse gear	**Plastic, contaminated**	To patronize, confront	To seek compliance
First gear	**Conditional**	To approve	To seek conformity
Second gear	**Encouraging**	To inform	To raise self-confidence
Third gear	**Affirming**	To affirm	To enhance self-motivation

Diagram 10.1 ▓ The four types of praise (1)

The different types of praise are further summarized as in Diagram 10.2 in terms of the four classroom types.

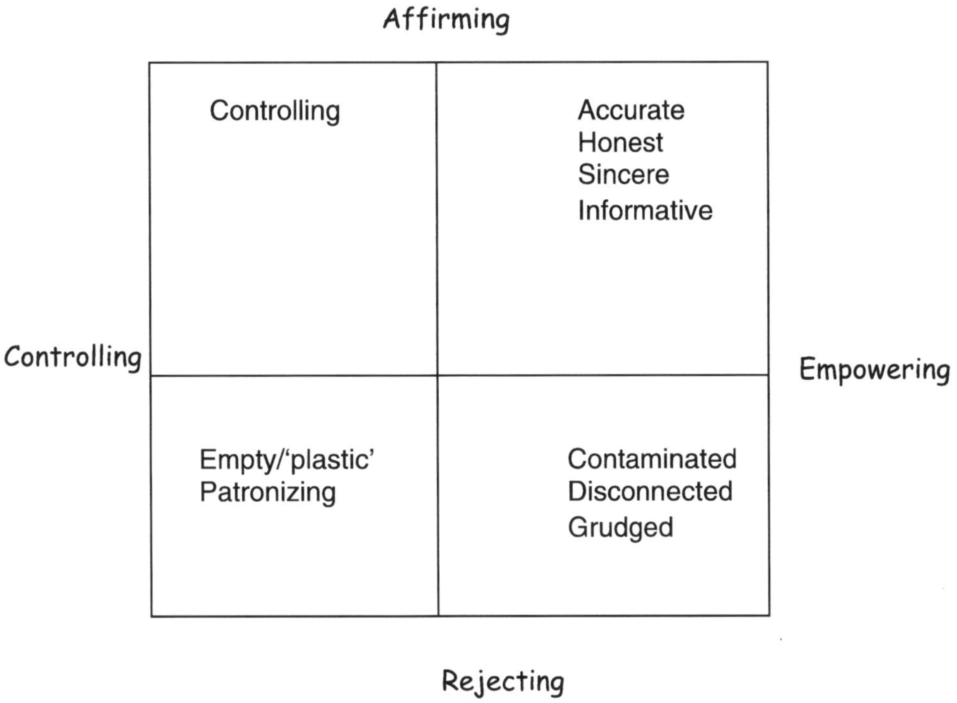

Affirming

Controlling	Accurate Honest Sincere Informative
Empty/'plastic' Patronizing	Contaminated Disconnected Grudged

Controlling

Empowering

Rejecting

Diagram 10.2 ■ The four types of praise (2)

Self-evaluation Checklists

These checklists summarize the main aspects of the four drivers, grouped in the four gears and provide a tool for self-evaluation.

Engagement

Reverse gear – context features creating insecurity and disengagement

- ☐ Underestimating students' capabilities
- ☐ Communicating negative expectations
- ☐ Focusing on student comparison
- ☐ Having favourites
- ☐ Emphasizing a 'prove yourself' approach
- ☐ Stressing the importance of ability as the main criterion of self-worth
- ☐ Conveying the idea that ability is fixed
- ☐ Showing no interest in students
- ☐ Not keeping promises
- ☐ Never admitting you are wrong
- ☐ Never listening to students
- ☐ Dismissing students' suggestions
- ☐ Using 'scare tactics' to motivate by fear or intimidation

First gear – foundations for a sense of security

☐ Teachers' emotions create resonance or positive feelings
☐ Communicating positive expectations
☐ Establishing rapport through both verbal and non-verbal communication
☐ Showing you want to get to know students
☐ Greeting each student by name
☐ Framing the tasks as learning processes rather than evaluations
☐ Stressing the value of effort while playing down the importance of ability
☐ Showing an interest and enjoyment in teaching
☐ Recognizing when students are not feeling well

Second gear – classroom processes that help shape a positive sense of identity

☐ Challenging limiting beliefs students have about their abilities while helping to choose a realistic challenge
☐ Helping students feel known and valued
☐ Creating an accepting, non-judgemental climate
☐ Students are known for their competence rather than their difficulties
☐ Encouraging students to develop their interests rather than please you
☐ Encouraging an 'improve yourself' rather than a 'prove yourself' approach
☐ Emphasizing the belief that students can and will do better
☐ Focusing on individual achievement rather than comparison
☐ Encouraging question-asking, risk-taking and expressing opinions
☐ Conveying how much everyone is learning
☐ Conveying the many ways to succeed
☐ Admitting mistakes, apologizing
☐ Asking students about their learning experiences and what helps them to learn best
☐ Valuing students' suggestions

Third gear – enhancing features that encourage self-determination

☐ Encouraging students to give positive feedback to each other
☐ Asking students about what helps them learn best
☐ Accepting feedback from students neutrally and calmly
☐ Communicating that students are known well and understood

Structure

Reverse gear – context features creating insecurity and disengagement

☐ Acting superior
☐ Emphasizing control more than the goals and purpose of learning
☐ Emphasizing discipline and control for its own sake
☐ Stressing doing what you are told
☐ Imposing excessive and negative rules
☐ Applying rules inconsistently
☐ Not following the rules yourself
☐ Trying to exercise control ambiguously
☐ Dominating and degrading students

☐ Creating uncertainty by not making clear the expected outcomes

First gear – foundations for a sense of security
☐ Providing a strong task orientation and moderate structure
☐ Setting limits in non-controlling ways
☐ Emphasizing the goals and purpose of learning rather than control
☐ Communicating rules and routines as a matter of instruction not control
☐ Applying rules, routines and penalties consistently
☐ Making the reasons for rules explicit and precise
☐ Expressing rules in terms of appropriate rather than prohibited behaviour
☐ Assuming authority and exercising control with unambiguous instructions
☐ Minimizing uncertainty in achievement by making clear the expected outcomes
☐ Providing consistency and predictability that let students know what to expect

Second gear – classroom processes that help shape a positive sense of identity
☐ While making students accountable, imposing authority to a minimum
☐ Helping students set realistic goals for themselves, their own time limits etc.
☐ Stressing sensible self-control rather than lots of petty instructions
☐ Recognizing the rights and feelings of students
☐ Negotiating learning objectives with the students as much as possible
☐ Negotiating rules with the students
☐ Showing a sense of humour, not taking self too seriously

Third gear – enhancing features that encourage self-determination
☐ Imposing authority to a minimum and maximizing student initiative
☐ Creating a less hierarchical, more equal teacher–student relationship
☐ Exchanging the role of teacher and learner routinely
☐ Allowing students to set their own rules
☐ Maximizing student initiative by giving students leadership roles, choices, a share of responsibilities and opportunities for decision-making
☐ Helping students develop skills that will enable them to take responsibility for their own learning and to solve their own problems
☐ Giving students discretion in setting schedules, work methods, the order in which they will work on tasks, when and how to check quality, when to start and stop, take breaks, prioritize, etc.

Stimulation

Reverse gear – context features creating insecurity and disengagement
☐ Setting unattainable goals
☐ Creating uncertainty through vague outcomes
☐ Encouraging students to set unrealistic goals
☐ Showing a lack of enthusiasm for the curriculum
☐ Failing to offer a clarity of purpose, personal relevance and meaningfulness
☐ Providing little stimulation and enjoyment
☐ Fostering a preference for easy work
☐ Lack of pace

☐ Doing everything for students
☐ Giving unsolicited help

First gear – foundations for a sense of security
☐ Showing enthusiasm for your curriculum
☐ Providing a clarity of purpose
☐ Setting goals which are perceived as attainable, appropriate
☐ Highlighting the importance and usefulness of the work
☐ Setting specific objectives with clear criteria for completion
☐ Increasing knowledge and understanding
☐ Providing stimulation and enjoyment
☐ Making sure students have realistic aspirations
☐ Taking the lead as the expert who gives information to passive learners
☐ Deciding on the curriculum content that is non-negotiable
☐ Organizing activities simultaneously, using differentiated materials
☐ Letting students work in changing groupings not necessarily defined by ability – to avoid student comparison

Second gear – classroom processes that help shape a positive sense of identity
☐ Creating curiosity through variety and diversity and by being surprising
☐ Allowing fantasy through the creation of imaginary circumstances
☐ Adapting teaching methods to students' learning styles
☐ Setting an optimal challenge, just ahead of skill level while permitting control
☐ Allowing students to perform to the limits of their ability
☐ Encouraging student engagement through problem-solving, role-playing and simulation
☐ Providing a sense of personal relevance and meaningfulness
☐ Relating the curriculum to students' own lives and experiences
☐ Focusing on what students are interested in and think is relevant and important
☐ Promoting a sense of competence, accomplishment and positive affect
☐ Emphasizing how students learn rather than checking performance
☐ Helping students to construct knowledge via participatory and discovery learning

Third gear – enhancing features that encourage self-determination
☐ Helping students to set realistic goals for themselves
☐ Offering students opportunities to solve problems
☐ Modelling attitudes such as, patience, persistence and using mistakes
☐ Helping students to construct own ways of processing knowledge and making it their own
☐ Encouraging critical investigation and a reorganization of knowledge
☐ Letting the students take control of their own learning as autonomous learners

Feedback

Reverse gear – context features creating insecurity and disengagement
☐ Showing impatience and frustration at mistakes

☐ Using excessive and judgemental criticism
☐ Being quick to criticize
☐ Emphasizing disapproval of the student as a person
☐ Giving unfair punishments
☐ Punishing everyone when you do not know who is to blame
☐ Personalizing punishment in a way that stresses blame and makes students pay for mistakes
☐ Using capricious discipline
☐ Giving empty, insincere praise
☐ Giving excessive praise for easy tasks
☐ Emphasizing rewards beforehand and distracting attention from the activities
☐ Using rewards to manipulate
☐ Defining success in terms of normative progress
☐ Showing pity
☐ Feedback disconnected from students' thinking
☐ Not offering any scope for dialogue
☐ Not giving suggestions for improvement
☐ Feedback centred on the teacher's needs and goals

First gear – foundations for a sense of security
☐ Not emphasizing rewards beforehand, and distracting attention from the activity
☐ Making rewards a natural part of the student–teacher relationship
☐ Making rewards explicit and instructive
☐ Giving punishment that has a clear purpose
☐ Giving punishment that is fair and follows reasonably from the behaviour
☐ Controlling all the feedback to passive learners
☐ Evaluating, pointing to the gap between student performance and desired outcome

Second gear – classroom processes that help shape a positive sense of identity
☐ Providing information about what went well and how students contributed
☐ Stressing personal improvement that helps students feel responsible for success
☐ Encouraging students to put down progress to student strategies and effort
☐ Attributing ownership of good ideas to students
☐ Encouraging students to put down failure to insufficient effort or inappropriate strategies
☐ Discouraging 'put downs', including self 'put downs'
☐ Emphasizing disapproval of the act, not the student
☐ Encouraging recovery by recognizing misbehaviour as a mistake
☐ Recognizing student effort
☐ Praising students for doing their best
☐ Treating mistakes as opportunities for learning and information about how students learn
☐ Giving students opportunities to correct mistakes before marking
☐ Giving sensitively clear and accurate reasons for failure and ways to overcome it
☐ Starting from and building on strengths to balance any negative comments
☐ Using moderate criticism to convey a belief that the student can do better
☐ Giving praise and other rewards to encourage rather than control

☐ Looking for reconciliation
☐ Looking for solutions not dwelling on past problems
☐ Allocating responsibility, to resolve a problem rather than blaming
☐ Helping students make connections in their understanding
☐ Describing rather than judging student performance
☐ Sharing your perspective on their performance to help student self-reflection
☐ Inviting a response from students

Third gear – enhancing features that encourage self-determination
☐ Making students feel responsible for their progress
☐ Training students to recognize their achievements
☐ Helping students apply their own criteria for progress
☐ Inviting students to suggest ways to improve
☐ Encouraging students to provide their own feedback
☐ Making feedback an integral part of class life
☐ Creating a dialogue with students on their performance
☐ Being less concerned with judgement and more with maximizing learning

Part IV

Summary and Conclusions

11 Motivating Boys and Girls

While this book has outlined general principles and processes involved in motivating all young people, it will be important to take into account a number of significant differences between the general motives and subsequent mindsets of boys and girls. Consequently there will be certain driver applications that may be particularly beneficial for boys and others for girls.

Male and Female Type Motives

The motivational profiles of boys and girls differ in some important ways (summarized in Table 11.1). These are differences in degree, in that the between-sex differences exceed the within-sex differences. There is, of course, a great deal of overlap between the distributions of features between the sexes as well as major differences within each gender.

Table 11.1 The key gender differences

	Girls	Boys
Self-definition	In terms of their relationships, group membership	Their unique features but also group membership, big groups/collective associations
Motives	Connectedness, approval of others, conform, fit in with others	Individuality, power over others, autonomy and control, status
Goals	Duty goals, multiple, balanced goals, general interests	Ideal goals, personal status, focused interest
Attitudes to achievement	Mastery, interest in hard work, success for its own sake	Performance/self-promotion, seek out what will bring recognition
Dealing with failure	Learned helplessness, personal attributions for failure	Protect self-worth by finding external reasons for failure, self-handicapping by not doing work, playing up, procrastinating, aiming too high or too low
Self-esteem	Contingent, acceptance on compliance, realistic, modest, susceptible to criticism, overassimilate criticism	Inflated, only interested in what leaders think, unrealistically high expectations, discount deficiencies they do not see as important or feel do not describe them, exaggerate unique abilities, risk-takers and attention-seekers
Peer group	Non-hierarchical, characterized by intimate friendship, co-operation	Hierarchical, combative, vie with each other for status, refrain from showing weakness, do not ask for help, group loyalty and collective skills

Girls' generally greater willingness to conform and fit in with others, together with their greater interest in hard work make them more likely to adjust better to school than boys. In particular and in relation to the motivation model, girls' goals relate to seeking intimacy and affirmation. School structures, curriculum and teaching methodologies are in general more 'girl friendly', for example the predominantly verbal and passive mode of curricular delivery. Of course, not all girls experience school positively. In contrast, however, schools can be particularly demotivating for large numbers of boys and find it harder to motivate boys (McLean, 2003). They find it particularly difficult to handle boys' need for individuality and autonomy.

Girls have less need for external structure as they can impose their own by, for example, creating their own rules. Boys are more vulnerable to behaviour problems related to undercontrol while girls are more likely to have personal problems of overcontrol, such as eating difficulties. Males value their individuality and power to impact on others, while females value intimacy with, and approval of, others. Whatever males do they invariably like to be ranked number one. Boys' greatest need is for empowerment through structure to mediate their need for autonomy, while for girls it is affirmation through involvement to mediate their need for intimacy and connectedness.

While Western culture values independence and autonomy and the demonstration of one's uniqueness and individuality as the basis of self-worth, schools prefer and promote conformity. This 'feminization' of school causes difficulty for boys and may also devalue schools for them.

This book argues that the ultimate goal of teaching is to help students reach the stage of self-determination by gradually supporting their autonomy. The challenge with girls is to encourage that sense of autonomy that does not come readily to them. Boys paradoxically have a greater desire for autonomy but also at the same time a greater dependency on external structures to mediate that autonomy.

Eventually, certain aspects of the male profile may help them succeed if they can adapt to the demands of school. Boys' ambition, relatively high self-esteem, competitiveness and ability to take a deep focused interest in topics can help them to achieve their potential. Females tend to have multiple goals and more balanced priorities, and so prefer to keep their interests more general. Clearly there are major social influences that need to be taken into account, but these motivational features may help explain in part why more boys fail and become disaffected but more boys also eventually become high achievers

Social Worlds

Belongingness is a fundamental need but males and females meet this need in different ways. Girls' upbringing and social roles encourage them to maintain close relationships. Females define themselves in terms of their close relationships, and work to maintain these connections (Cross and Madson, 1997). Males' socialization and roles emphasize more collective aspects of the social world and they prefer large group associations. Males' self-definition is generally based on their individuality and they are interested in enhancing their personal status within large groups. They are attuned to group aspects of social relationships, have great group loyalty and collective skills, describe themselves in collective terms and are motivated to support their groups (Gabriel and Gardner, 1999).

The main motive for girls is to seek close relationships and so they develop the ability to take the perspective of others and, as a consequence, will be more likely to fit in to serve the needs of others. In contrast boys' main motive is to distinguish themselves from others. Males have a significantly higher desire for control than females (Burger, 1990). A common example of female accommodation and male control might be the male domination of the television remote control in most living rooms.

Gender roles for males and females prescribe different qualities. Parents have been found to control boys but also at the same time give them room for autonomy. In contrast they tend to be controlling all the time with girls (Maccoby and Martin, 1983). Boys are encouraged to be assertive and self-promoting, while girls are not encouraged to boast about themselves. Boys and girls develop different ways of interacting within the predominant single-sex peer group and, when they do mix, the boys' strategies tend to prevail, leaving girls feeling less competent, important or powerful.

From an early age girls' groups are typically characterized by intimate friendship and cooperation (Whiting and Edwards, 1973). Girls' groups are less hierarchical. Leadership in a group of girls can be problematic and may be seen as being stuck-up or bossy. Girls tend on the whole not to boss each other around and they prefer to co-operate and negotiate. The most influential girls are the ones who get the most attention from others. Boys' groups in contrast are characterized by competition, dominating behaviour, more combative relationships and tend to have a more hierarchical structure (Maltz and Borker, 1983). There is a leader who tells the others what to do. Boys vie with each other for status and so refrain from showing any weakness. They do not like to ask for help (or directions!) because they do not want anyone to know they are in difficulty.

▨ Attitudes to Achievement and Explanations of Progress

Because of their main motives, girls are more likely to adopt a mastery attitude towards achievement and will be more interested in learning according to self-set standards (Licht and Dweck, 1984; Lightbody et al., 1996). Their main goal will be to learn and increase their skills, reflected by, for example, their greater willingness to ask for help. Boys are more likely to have a performance attitude with a focus on relative ability and how ability will be judged, for example the boy who always wants to be first in line and best at everything. The main goal is to perform well to show capability of a particular skill. They are concerned about their ability and try to show they are smarter than others (Whiting and Edwards, 1973). Males respond more to any competitive or challenge cues in the classroom and are more likely to adopt a self-promotion attitude by focusing on their successes while denying their failures (Maccoby and Jacobsen, 1974), exaggerating their abilities and showing off (Whiting and Edwards, 1973).

Some males have to win at all costs and, so, may be more likely to cheat. Males tend to seek out what will bring them recognition rather than look for feedback that will improve their performance. They tend to be motivated by anything that signals the desired group status, such as points, stars and other status symbols.

The performance attitude will lead some boys to be motivated by a fear of failure. When driven by fear of failure their main goal will be to protect their self-worth and to try to retain control of the situation. As showing ability is important for boys, they adopt a defensive externalizing approach when their ability is called into question. They do this by blaming other things to explain poor performance, by, for example, putting failure down to bad luck and other factors like teacher attitude (Dweck and Bush, 1976). Or they use self-handicapping strategies like not doing work and playing up in class, or applying defence mechanisms such as procrastination, or aiming too high or too low (Thompson, 1999). Such boys often present a 'couldn't care less front' and delude themselves that they could be successful if they could only be bothered and stopped 'messing about'.

Girls also have a fear of failure that is expressed perhaps more often in the form of helplessness (Dweck et al., 1978). Girls tend to make more personal attributions for failure than boys. They may be more likely to view failure as evidence of low ability and to give up trying.

Self-esteem

Everyone is motivated to maintain self-esteem, but because of their different motives, the sources of self-esteem vary between boys and girls. Therefore, they use different strategies to protect, maintain and enhance their self-worth. Boys are more interested in individuality, autonomy and control, while girls are more concerned about being involved with and approved of by others. Consequently, for boys a loss of a sense of autonomy may damage self-esteem, while conflict or damage to significant relationships is more likely to threaten girls' self-esteem.

Gender differences in self-esteem increase with age. Around the start of and continuing throughout secondary school, self-esteem is consistently lower for females (King *et al.*, 1999). Decreased perceptions of attractiveness would appear to contribute to their lowered self-esteem. Self-perception of physical competence in boys and physical condition in girls are essentially related to favourable life adjustment. Although the media increasingly emphasizes the importance of appearance for males, there is still more latitude in the standards of attractiveness for males. Moreover, for males there is not the single focus on looks as the way to acceptance and self-esteem that prevails for females.

Females are more likely to suffer depression and anxiety, possibly because of the more complex issues with which they have to grapple and because they are more prone to experience guilt when they do not live up to their own and others' standards (Nolen-Hoeksema, 1990; 1995; Nolen-Hoeksema and Girgus, 1994; Nolen-Hoeksema, Girgus and Seligman, 1995). Females are more likely to adopt duty goals, for example sending birthday or Christmas cards (Higgins, 1991). In the classroom girls will be more likely to comply with instructions. Because self-esteem is so dependent for females on how they look and how they comply with and meet others' needs, and because they are brought up to see themselves as objects of judgement, contingent self-esteem is perhaps likely to be more prevalent among girls than boys. Girls growing up are judged heavily on something over which they have little control, but which is linked to their self-esteem, namely, their appearance.

In contrast boys' self-evaluations are less influenced by what others think of them, except for the leaders of their group. They can in fact self-enhance in the face of negative feedback, exaggerate their abilities to appear better than others and tend to think their abilities are unique. For example, boys generally think they are more intelligent (Beyer, 1990; 1999) and more physically competent than females (Van Wersch, 1997). Consequently, inflated self-esteem is perhaps likely to be more prevalent among boys. Females tend to be more realistic or modest and also more likely to make positive comments about others (Roberts, 1991). Females, for example, tend to underestimate their intelligence. Parents are more controlling of their daughters than their sons and this may further help explain the difference between the genders in how they appraise themselves.

Gender-Specific Driver Applications

Engagement

Because of the above factors, it is important to try to encourage in boys a mastery attitude by emphasizing an 'improve yourself' rather than a 'prove yourself' approach to learning. The teacher can do this by communicating how much everyone is learning and that there are many ways to succeed. Students are encouraged to recognize their own strengths and put success down to their skills and effort, and any failure to not enough effort or inappropriate strategies rather than to a lack of ability.

The classroom organization needs to avoid focusing attention on comparison between students and make perceptions of ability less salient to achievement. In a competitive climate characterized by judgemental comparison, boys will be reluctant to risk putting their ability on the line. Opportunities should be provided for students to learn mainly with each other, instead of against or apart from each other, and to work with peers in a variety of changing groupings. Boys need to be particularly encouraged to give positive feedback to each other, take responsibility for their own and others' learning and to co-operate rather than compete.

A competitive situation, however, is a good way to find challenges that can be stimulating for boys who are more comfortable when comparisons are made between themselves and their peers, as in quizzes. When given a choice, boys prefer competitive to co-operative games. Boys will feel good when such comparisons highlight their superiority. Girls feel better when comparison highlights similarity with their classmates. Excessive competition should be avoided, however, as it encourages boys to strive for selfish goals and teaches them that other students are obstacles to success. It reinforces the natural inclinations of boys to be self-centred and hierarchical. Competition that does not degrade others, however, can be beneficial for boys, for example in a pairs or group competition.

Structure

In relation to getting the best from boys, the great challenge for teachers is to strike a happy medium between controlling them and seeking their compliance while releasing their potential and need for self-determination. This tension can be resolved, as discussed earlier, by imposing authority then gradually, in a geared approach, letting go of the reins and providing increasing opportunities for negotiation, choice and responsibilities. Empowerment requires, in the first instance, authoritative teachers who give a sense of direction, reasonable pressure and increasing choice within limits set in non-controlling ways.

Boys will dominate groups from the start of schooling, will be less ready to conform and will be more reluctant to bow to teacher authority. They will challenge teachers who may respond by becoming overcontrolling and limit their self-expression and creativity. Boys who come into the class with a low level of motivation will push the teacher into the reverse gear of 'excessive power assertion'. 'Power assertion' is the starting point for any motivating relationship with a group of boys and is characterized by firm fairness. The transition to 'Power-sharing' is the most important and challenging phase in the development of a motivating classroom for boys and involves mutual respect. Boys' greater need for external structure can be met with an emphasis on fairness and transparency, a clear sense of direction, time limits and clear rules. Boys need autonomy within a supportive rather than coercive structure. If boys are not given the supportive structure and autonomy they need, some will react with disruptive behaviour.

Essentially, when the self-esteem of boys is threatened, they may act out against the authority figure. Girls learn early on in life that they cannot retaliate so readily, and so they develop adaptive responses to this power imbalance, which are invariably indirect and can be regarded as manipulative. In a similar way, girls develop more subtle methods of challenging authority. They learn to disguise their hostility towards teachers by, for example, gossiping about them or making up a funny nickname that they share with the peer group. They will maintain their self-esteem in subtle non-confrontational ways by, for example, neutralizing a teacher's criticism by playing up to it. They discover they have a lot of scope for dealing obliquely with authority, for example by feigning illness to avoid physical education classes.

Stimulation

Girls have a greater tendency towards fear of failure and need to be certain before they will commit themselves. Consequently, they can be more reluctant to answer questions, although they are more likely to know the answer. Girls will be more threatened by whole-class questioning sessions. Boys, on the other hand, are greater risk-takers and attention-seekers who will dominate such sessions. This example indicates the importance of having gender-balanced groupings to accommodate the strengths and weaknesses of each gender. Setting advance prompts for gender-balanced grouping can allow girls' more reflective style to balance boys' impulsivity, while the boys' confidence may encourage and energize the girls.

Doing well depends as much on students choosing a realistic level of challenge as it does on ability. Students need to make realistic judgements about their own capacity relative to the demands of the task. Many boys hold unrealistically high expectations for themselves and teachers can mistakenly praise such unrealistic aspirations as evidence of their willingness to try hard and, so, unwittingly reinforce goals that are destined to lead to disappointment. It is more helpful to encourage an accurate match between boys' aspirations and their current skills so boys will benefit from tasks being broken down into achievable steps.

Feedback

Females tend to pay more attention and respond more discriminately to feedback and, so, are more influenced by it than boys (Roberts, 1991). Although, overall, boys tend to be given more feedback (Minuchin and Shapiro, 1983), the feedback they receive is more likely to be negative (Etangl and Harlow, 1975) and more about their behaviour and motivation (Brophy and Good, 1970). Feedback given to girls tends to be more related to their ability (Dweck *et al.*, 1978). Boys also give each other more negative feedback within their dominance-led and combative peer relationships (Maltz and Borker, 1983).

Girls, however, may be more vulnerable to criticism, both direct and implied. Boys can more readily discount criticism and will think it does not describe them correctly. Girls tend more to overassimilate negative feedback into their view of themselves and are less able to point to alternative positive qualities. The tendency to broaden a specific criticism into a general sense of failure reflects, perhaps, females' self-identity goals compared with males' more pragmatic goals. Any negative feedback to girls needs to be balanced with reminders of other positive aspects and reassurances that the problems can be remedied. It is crucial to distinguish disapproval of their behaviour or their work from them as a person. In contrast, arrogant boys need to be criticized in ways which counter their capacity to discount deficiencies which they do not see as important and in ways which stress that the criticism is accurate, justified and important.

Punishments will be less necessary with girls, but when used will be more likely to have the desired impact. Punishment is particularly problematic with boys who often put up a greater resistance by displaying, for example, an 'I'll show you can't hurt me' mentality. Public punishment can often lead to boys challenging the teacher. It is often more effective to reprimand or punish a boy in private and so give less incentive to challenge the teacher. If a boy appears unaffected by the teacher's punishment it will be important that the teacher does not become more frustrated and react with escalating anger. Some punishments do no more than provide boys with much needed status within the peer group. On the other hand, getting into trouble does not play well within most female peer groups. Girls are more likely to be humiliated by punishment, which they find highly embarrassing. Girls, consequently find group reprimands or punishments less demeaning.

It is harder to find opportunities to praise boys and it is often wrongly thought that boys are resistant to praise or that boys do not need praise as much as girls. We all benefit from praise. Indeed if boys feel they have worked hard and do not get any acknowledgement they will be more likely to be put off. Younger boys like public acclaim from teachers but by the secondary stage boys place less value on teacher approval. Indirect praise, given obliquely or quietly in private, will work best with older boys. Girls are usually happy with direct and explicit praise. Given boys' need for external structure, more immediate and more regular feedback will be particularly advantageous with boys.

12 The Motivating School

Introduction

This book has concentrated on how teachers can provide optimal learning opportunities. Such classrooms, however, are more likely to be found within a school where the leadership operates the motivating principles outlined here and applies these principles to motivate the teaching staff (Maehr, 1991; Maehr and Midgeley, 1996). School leaders play a critical role in the development of motivating schools. Effective managers understand the importance of linking whole-school development and effectiveness with individual teacher growth and efficacy (Senge *et al.*, 1994).

Just as teachers 'download' their mindsets to students via their classroom practice, so school managers, at the top of the 'motivation chain', 'download' their mindsets to their staff. The model and principles outlined here about motivating students apply equally well to how management should seek to understand and get the best from their teaching colleagues. It goes without saying that the classroom applications can also be used within a whole-school context. School managers are recommended to reconsider these chapters from their management perspective. For example, the model can be applied to how schools communicate and work with parents (Askew, 2000), or to how new members of staff are inducted and mentored.

Leadership

This book argues that schools need management teams that have the vision to move from a control culture to an emphasis on self-motivation and to encourage the optimistic view that learning is an intrinsic part of human nature that needs to be nurtured. Management will achieve this through the four drivers; for example:

- *Engagement.* High performance schools have been found to have headteachers who are more likely to adopt a flexible and resonant style while headteachers in lower-performing schools have a more rigid dissonant style (Hay Group, 2000). The more effective schools benefit from *transformational* leadership that is based on equity and collegiality (affirmation). Transformational leaders engage colleagues' thoughts and feelings and capture their imagination.

  Motivating managers strive to build up reserves in their colleagues' emotional bank account (Covey, 1990) with deposits made through courtesies, noticing their strengths and listening to them, and seeking to understand them. They balance imposing their point of view with consideration for colleagues' views. Even small displays of disrespect can make large withdrawals. Headteachers who have not made many deposits can not afford to make many withdrawals.

- *Stimulation.* Visionary heads help colleagues see how their work fits into the big picture and so give clarity and a sense of purpose (Burns, 1978). They are good at delegating and giving challenging tasks that stretch colleagues in contrast to unhelpful 'dumping' of unachievable tasks. They encourage staff to go on training courses and embrace the knowledge they bring back.

- *Structure.* Transformational leaders give a clear vision and a sense of direction (empowerment). They distribute and share as much information as possible and transform the school culture by taking everyone along with them at every stage. Transactional leaders, in contrast, hold on to their power through conditional deals they make with staff. Heads of lower-performing schools tend to be trapped in the hierarchical control mentality (Hay Group, 2000).

■ *Feedback.* The empathic style of transformational leaders means they listen to colleagues before giving feedback and encourage an open two-way sharing of thoughts and emotions. The relationships transactional leaders have with colleagues are characterized by deals that seek co-operation and loyalty in return for rewards.

The key features of the drivers of each leadership style are compared in Table 12.1.

Table 12.1 Transactional and transformational leadership

Transactional leadership	Transformational leadership
Engagement	
Dissonant style,	Resonant style,
conditional deals,	open sharing,
favouritism	equity and collegiality
Structure	
Holds on to power,	Shares information,
hierarchical decision-making,	participative decision-making,
dumps unachievable tasks	delegates challenging tasks
Stimulation	
No sense of direction,	Sense of direction,
reactive	shows the big picture,
	clarity and sense of purpose
Feedback	
Uses rewards	Listens before giving feedback,
to seek co-operation	two-way dialogue

Transactional leaders are in first or reverse gear on some drivers, while the transformational leaders operate in second and third gear across the four drivers.

Major differences in management styles have been found in school exclusion research that distinguishes more and less inclusive schools (McLean, 1987; Munn and Lloyd, 2000). Inclusive management saw the school's responsibility as developing the social and academic achievement of all students while less inclusive schools narrowed their remit to the academic progress of conforming students. Consequently, low-excluding schools had a more flexible curriculum, more staff support, involved in-house and outside support in joint problem-solving, including decisions on exclusions, and built non-judgemental relations with parents. High-excluding schools concentrated almost exclusively on the academic curriculum, preferred extraction and wanted external agencies to 'fix' problem students or place them elsewhere. They had hierarchical decision-making procedures regarding exclusions. They blamed problem students for a lot of their concerns and expected unquestioning parental support.

Individual classroom climates contribute to, but are also shaped by, the school culture that provides the guiding beliefs that pervade the school, the spirit that motivates ideas and practices. Management's expectations and behaviour are central to the establishment of a motivating culture that fosters mastery attitudes towards achievement and nurtures intrinsic motivation. Management is responsible for instilling in the teachers the key beliefs that students can and will learn and for encouraging optimistic ambitions for their students. Schools that appear to be successful, despite significant disadvantages, have an optimistic and inclusive philosophy that all students can succeed despite the odds (Maden and Hillman, 1996).

School management also needs to have an overview of class teachers' motivational strategies across the school and throughout the different stages in order to:

▓ maintain some consistency of student experience

▓ allow class strategies to become increasingly sophisticated as students move up the school, to facilitate the idea of a staged progression of trust that provides increasing opportunities for negotiation, choice and responsibilities

▓ to intervene when necessary in problematic interactions between students and teachers.

The Management Motive

A central factor that separates constructive from unsupportive heads is their contrasting motives for control. All of us are highly motivated to exercise control over our lives. Some people are keen to control others. Such people often appear similar to those with positive self-esteem in that they feel capable and optimistic. They will probably have had positive experiences of exercising control over important life events that will have helped contribute to their feelings of competency (Burger, 1990; 1992). They experience what could be termed *autonomous* control. On the other hand, for others, exercising control may be a way of combating feelings of chaos or helplessness, or of maintaining their fragile self-esteem (Brown, 1988; West and Prinz, 1987). They fight their feelings by striving to exercise control over other aspects of their lives. This could be called *chaos-avoidance* control.

Some people with a high desire for control will satisfy this need through leadership positions and become headteachers. The management style of such people will be a function of how their desire for control has developed throughout their lives. Those whose leadership drive is based on a healthy self-esteem and *autonomous* control show confidence, trust and respect in their working relationships.

In contrast, those whose desire for control is based on chaos-driven control or is driven by fragile self-esteem may have a tendency to be overdominant, rigid or manipulative in their relationships with colleagues. Difficulty with trusting people combined with a high desire for control may not be that uncommon. A link has been found between desire for control and suspiciousness (Fenigstein and Vanable, 1992). An excessive need for power over others has been found to have the same effect as being highly stressed (McClelland, 1980). Such people, especially those with a highly competitive attitude to achievement can be drawn, like moths to a flame, to the top posts.

This particular set of motivation mindsets will tend to be downloaded to their staff through a bullying or interfering management culture. People with high esteem actively scapegoat others with whom they can compare favourably (Gibbons and McCoy, 1991), and ridicule out-group members (Crocker and Major, 1989; Crocker and Luhtonen, 1990). Such headteachers may marginalize anyone who disagrees with them while showing favouritism to others. They may 'dump' unachievable tasks on colleagues or remove responsibilities from others. They do not encourage staff to attend courses, ridicule anyone paying for themselves and belittle colleagues who return knowing more than they do, by, for example, excluding them from working groups.

Those attracted to leadership to meet their own needs rather than apply their skills allow their needs to take priority over everyone else's needs. The enhancement of their personal status becomes their guiding principle. Their interactions with others are geared to achieving their own agenda rather than supporting teachers to meet their own particular and collective goals. They need to be centre stage and cannot put their ego to one side long enough to work for the common cause. While teachers tell pupils not to interrupt, some headteachers expect an instant response from the teacher in front of the class.

Both contingent and unstable self-esteem suggest fragile feelings of worth that have a tenuous and pressured quality. Such leaders will be driven by their feelings that ebb and flow with their successes and failures. Self-esteem instability leads to favourable reactions to positive events and defensive reactions to negative events. Such esteem is a precious commodity that must be continually promoted in order to survive, and this makes them highly vulnerable to challenge which, in turn, creates defensiveness and self-aggrandizement. Consequently, such managers will have a heightened tendency to invest their self-worth and be ego-involved in and to overidentify with the job. The trouble is the more one's self-esteem is based in one particular domain, the more vulnerable it is (Crocker and Wolfe, 2001).

Staff Affirmation and Empowerment

Affirmation

Headteachers' attitudes and behaviour towards staff reflect and shape the quality of a school's inclusive ethos. Any cynical influence in the staffroom must in part be a reflection of what support the management team has offered. The power entrusted in headteachers needs to be exercised with sensitivity and respect. Student-centred teaching needs teacher-centred management, and management at all levels needs to treat teachers the same way they rightly expect teachers to treat their students.

The motivating school is one where teachers and other members of staff know that management is interested in them, what they are doing well and how they can improve. The school has an affirming culture that encourages among staff self-improvement, autonomy and a sense of relatedness. The climate facilitates involvement with and approval of others, encourages peer group support and offers role models as an integral part of school life. Classroom assistants and school auxiliaries are also seen to be providers of the four drivers for students.

In such schools, continuous professional learning is seen as a 'liberator' for staff, motivating them to cope more confidently with change.

Empowerment

Teachers and non-teaching staff in the motivating school know where the school is going and what the priority goals are. The management team is seen as trustworthy, knowledgeable and approachable, and so sets an empowering structure. The headteacher will give a clear sense of direction and exert reasonable pressure while giving choice within limits. The teachers feel they share power with management and have some autonomy within their own areas of responsibility. A culture of leadership is fostered throughout the school by giving staff at all levels leadership roles and responsibilities in accordance with their strengths, skills and remit.

Teachers have optimal motivation when they have achievable and specific goals to attain, feel confident about performing well and hold realistic aspirations, when the goals are appropriate and legitimate and a convincing rationale is given. Their teaching tasks allow performing to the limits of their ability. Teachers' duties provide variety and diversity, clarity of purpose, personal relevance and meaningfulness. They give staff a chance to solve problems and invite participation in making decisions. These features promote among staff a sense of competence, accomplishment and high morale.

Teacher appraisal is mainly through a process of self-evaluation. Feedback is provided that indicates progress and allows success to be attributed by teachers to their efforts and good use of planning and strategy.

One of the problems that headteachers have is finding time to listen to their colleagues, let alone to find out what motivates them. Yet few things are more motivating than personal attention from one's line manager. It is the best way of communicating the message that each member of staff matters. It also enables a key management task of helping develop teachers' sense of competency. A poor working relationship with a superior has been found to be a major cause of low motivation (Wilkins and Head, 2002). Management can help nurture feelings of involvement by making sure all staff are given recognition from time to time, by valuing all achievements, talking to staff about how they feel and what they think, allowing staff to express their opinions and concerns, and showing an interest in their lives outwith school.

Management Mindsets and Drivers

School management displays its own motivation mindsets via the external drivers it provides to its staff. Some examples of management mindsets and drivers are listed below.

Mindsets

▓ *Ideas about ability*:

Sees staff development as a way of improving.

Committed to lifelong learning.

▓ *Attitudes to achievement*:

Seeks out new challenges for self.

Seeks feedback so they can improve.

▓ *Explanations for progress*:

Puts success down to factors under the school's control.

Puts failure down to factors that can be rectified.

▓ *Self-efficacy*:

Sets positive goals.

Conveys a confident and decisive manner.

Copes well with setbacks.

Finds ways round obstacles.

Drivers

▓ *Engagement*:

Spends time building relationships with colleagues.

Treats colleagues with respect.

Works hard at building a cohesive team.

▓ *Stimulation*:

Puts forward new ideas aimed at improvement.

Suggests good ideas that stimulate innovation.

Encourages staff to take risks and develop new approaches.

Challenges and stretches colleagues.

▓ *Structure*:

Is able to communicate how things fit together.

Plans and co-ordinates the work of the team.

Helps colleagues set achievable goals.

Is able to balance priorities.

Gives clarity of purpose and sense of direction.

Ensures that policies emerge from all levels of the school.

■ *Feedback*:

Listens to colleagues before giving feedback.

Gives regular feedback to colleagues on their work.

Engages in a two-way dialogue.

The Motivating School Culture

The school culture can be analysed in terms of the four drivers.

Engagement

A motivating school culture encourages a mastery attitude by emphasizing an 'improve yourself' rather than a 'prove yourself' approach to learning, task mastery rather than performance, the learning process more than the product. It encourages question asking and risk-taking.

The motivating school sets a welcoming climate for all students. In such a setting negative labelling is avoided by promoted members of staff.

A mixture of competition and co-operation is used with students learning mainly with, instead of against or apart from each other. Excessive competition is avoided. Students' alliances into informal groups are usually made on the basis of academic performance and motivation for school, and such groups will have a major influence on how students view themselves and their attitudes to learning. School management has to find ways to discourage comparison between students as well as opportunities for students to work in a variety of changing groups, not necessarily defined by ability, so that perceptions of ability are made less salient to achievement.

Stimulation

The school communicates through whole-school activities such as school assemblies and award ceremonies how much everyone is learning, that there are many ways to succeed and that students who are less academically able are equally valued. All opportunities are taken to convey the beliefs to all students that ability is not fixed and that they can and will be successful.

Structure

The lead given by management should emphasize the goals and purpose of learning rather than discipline and control. Students need consistency of rules and routines for a sense of security. Consistency between teachers is something of an elusive butterfly, and difficult to achieve given the personal nature of much of teaching. This is particularly challenging with regard to those aspects shaped by the teacher's temperament, such as their style of conveying authority, setting their classroom climate, reprimanding and managing confrontations. Consistency at a corporate level should, however, be more achievable in terms of the use of rules and subsequent rewards and punishments. The goal for school management should be a unity of purpose within a diversity of practice. Consistency is a goal towards which schools will strive continuously without ever achieving the final goal.

The headteacher and senior staff need to give students leadership roles and a share of responsibilities and opportunities for decision-making to foster active participation and a sense of ownership in the school. Students need help to develop the skills that will enable them to take responsibility for their own learning. Schools are increasingly setting up opportunities to listen and consult meaningfully with students. Students, however, need to be trained and supported in this process from an early stage. Token efforts will not be fruitful.

Feedback

A motivating school makes exchanging feedback a natural part of school life and encourages students to seek feedback from the teacher and each other. To create such a climate, senior management needs to look for and be open to feedback from colleagues and students to help school improvement. It should be made clear that feedback is welcomed, by talking regularly with students and asking them what it is like being in this school.

A school's use of punishments is a key indicator of the integrity and maturity of its culture. Management has to give clarity and certainty over the role of punishment within school policies. At the same time the arsenal of whole-school rewards should reflect the school's core values and serve as a guide and encouragement to all students. The purpose of school award ceremonies needs careful consideration, particularly the intended messages they aim to communicate to students. Inclusive schools need to celebrate all students' progressions, regardless of their destinations (Mannion, 2002).

The Physical Environment

The physical climate is an important factor in the creation of the overall school ethos. High-performance buildings, as they have been termed, have been found to have better outcomes because of the better physical facilities, particularly acoustics, lighting, air quality and ventilation (Eley Associates, 2001). Such schools are designed to be pleasant and effective places to work, increasing both student and teacher satisfaction. They offer safe and secure environments that have, in particular, large amounts of natural daylight. Students and teachers can hear each other without shouting, and noise is minimized. Teachers can keep temperature and humidity in the 'comfort zone' and so avoid hot, stuffy or cold classrooms.

Working conditions, while found to have limited motivating power can be very demotivating if they are not right (Herzberg, Mausner and Synderman, 1959). These hygiene factors do not create higher levels of motivation but their negative features cause dissatisfaction. Good classroom conditions are an essential prerequisite to enable a focus on the motivating aspects of teaching and learning.

13 Summary and Conclusions

This final chapter summarizes the main arguments, recaps on the drivers and mindsets, and, finally, draws some conclusions.

Motivating from Inside

Motivation for learning comes ideally from inside. Self-motivation is a door that can only be unlocked from the inside. Students are on the lookout for information about the self that shapes their thoughts that, in turn, are the main driving forces behind their approach to learning. Teachers cannot motivate students directly but self-motivation paradoxically cannot be achieved alone and needs support from teachers. Teachers and schools spend an ever-increasing amount of effort trying to directly motivate students from the outside. A more effective approach is to motivate from the inside by using students' positive states to draw them into learning. This book has argued that schools can readily impact upon the key motivation mindsets.

The mindsets

Students think about their ability in two different ways. Those students who see intelligence as a fixed trait, as something they only have so much of and about which there is nothing they can do, hold an *entity* theory. Those who, in contrast, have an *incremental* view think it can be increased through effort. These *ideas about ability* lead students to interpret their progress in ways that can make some vulnerable and others robust in the face of setbacks and challenges.

Entity-type thinking probably exerts more and more negative influence on students as they go through school, making them more sensitive to anything that conveys information about their ability (Nicholls, Patashnick and Nolen, 1985; Rholes, Newman and Ruble, 1990). For most students it is ability, not effort that counts the most, and it counts more and more as they grow older, magnified by competition and by the fact that coursework is increasingly grouped by ability. Teacher assessments of student ability differences, for example, have been found to be stable (Cooper and McIntyre, 1996). However, an incremental view of ability can be fostered in schools by, for example, conveying how much everyone is learning and the many ways to succeed. Student beliefs about the multidimensional and dynamic nature of their talent can be strengthened by providing them with evidence of their own growth and development through time.

Students' attributions or *explanations of their progress* are crucial factors in shaping their competence beliefs. The motivational power of attributions comes from where they lie along four dimensions. *Locus* concerns whether a cause is seen as being internal or external to the student. *Stability* refers to whether the cause is stable or unstable across situations and over time. *Breadth* ranges from global to specific. *Controllability* suggests how much control a student has over a cause.

Besides specific goal-setting processes, students hold *attitudes to achievement* that form an integrated set of beliefs that lead to different ways of approaching and responding to learning situations. Students with a *mastery* attitude want to learn, increase ability and achieve *their* best compared to those with a *performance* attitude who are motivated to perform, display ability and to be *the* best. Mastery is in many ways the ideal, characterized by the twin concerns of achieving success rather than avoiding failure, as well as achieving mastery rather than showing oneself to be better than others. Failure-avoiding students may either feel *helpless* and give up, or adopt *self-protective* strategies when poor performance is anticipated and likely to reflect low ability, and when there are no excuses to let them 'off the hook'.

Self-esteem is our overall view of the degree to which we feel ourselves to be 'OK', dependent on our criteria for 'OK'. Although confused with self-efficacy or competence beliefs, it may be useful to consider it as different from self-efficacy beliefs that are based on judgements about abilities in specific areas. Self-esteem is more a global affective judgement of our general worth than an appraisal of competence in a particular area.

Self-esteem and its role in motivating learning may be better understood when considered along with the motivation mindsets with which it is intertwined. It may also be usefully considered as two-tiered: first, as a permeating process in terms of global self-worth and, secondly, as a contextual appraisal of specific capability. Self-esteem is an asset rather than an essential for motivating learning and it is more productive for schools to focus on what they can most readily affect.

The most important 'feel-good' factor is *self-efficacy in goal achievement* – the 'SEGA' factor! Particularly useful in boosting confidence is achieving goals that help us realize aspects of our ideal self.

The primary cause of disengagement from learning is repeatedly putting failure down to stable, personal, uncontrollable and global factors that suggest failure is inevitable. Students with a lethal cocktail of pessimistic explanations of progress, fixed ability ideas, a strong performance attitude to achievement and low competency beliefs are especially vulnerable to a spiral of failure avoidance.

The tendency to prefer mastery self-referenced evaluations of progress is more likely to maintain positive self-esteem. If a person has a mastery attitude and is not progressing as well as others he or she can still have positive self-esteem, unlike someone with a competitive attitude who will have high esteem only if he or she is doing well. Not every student can be high in ability, but they can all be high in mastery attitudes.

The drivers

A major challenge for schools is to balance the need students have for acceptance and accurate feedback. Motivating teachers achieve this through the gears of the relationship dimension and move from conditional acceptance through recognition to affirmative feedback, to signal that they know the students well and value them and their efforts.

A second challenge is to strike a happy medium between seeking compliance while realizing students' potential for self-determination. This can be resolved by imposing authority without coercion, then providing gradually in a geared progression of trust more and more opportunities for negotiation, choice and responsibilities. Power assertion can thus be transformed into personal power via power-sharing.

The two interacting processes of relationships (affirmation) and power (empowerment) construct the framework of the driver model. The school culture allocates rewards and exercises power over students, and so socializes and controls students through its routines and rituals (Etzioni, 1996). How motivating a school is will be determined by the nature of its drivers. Two drivers within the classroom form the relationship dimension and achieve the socialisation function. First, *engagement* lets students know that the teacher wants to get to know them. Secondly, *feedback* tells students how well they are doing. The motivating classroom also needs the power dimension that is achieved principally through *stimulation* from motivating goals and activities and *structure*, that is, the amount of explicit information available about how to achieve effectively the classroom goals.

Engagement and feedback are the essential elements of the teacher–student relationship. Engagement is the process whereby teachers get to know students as much as possible as individual personalities. This, in turn, allows them to be responsive to students' needs and give formative feedback. Being autonomy-supportive means valuing students for who they are and acknowledging their feelings and points of view. Engagement benefits greatly from self-disclosure. For some students, however, this is a risky business and they prefer to keep to themselves or put on a calculated display of the self rather than exposing their real self.

Demotivating teachers show little interest in students, make it obvious they do not know the students well but jump to conclusions quickly about them and make inappropriate personal comments. Teachers with low expectations and pessimistic assumptions complain about their pupils' low motivation yet fail to see the connection between their own mindsets and their pupils' apathy.

Personalized feedback has the danger of feeding a fragile self-esteem, making students feel good when they are praised but bad when they are criticized. If a student, for example, is told repeatedly that he or she is bad he or she will assume an entity theory of personality, believe he or she is bad and that he or she cannot change.

Teacher comments are best focused upon students' individual progress and actions. Thus the teacher tunes into the whole person and provides individualized feedback but avoids making personal comments. This is the essence of an affirming relationship that sets the context whereby teachers maximize their impact on the student mindsets.

Diagram 13.1 summarizes the key elements of teacher attitudes in the four contexts created by two interacting dimensions. The dimensions are, first, inclusive versus rejecting attitudes and, secondly, motivated by fear of losing power versus motivated to seek co-operation.

Inclusive attitudes

Plastic praise Pity Unsolicited help Easy work	Optimism, trust
Command storm Label trap Blame-throwing Fault-finding 'Killer' feedback	Ah but … why can't you … It's never good enough Contaminated praise 'Scare tactics'

Motivated by fear of losing power (left)   **Motivated to seek co-operation** (right)

Rejecting

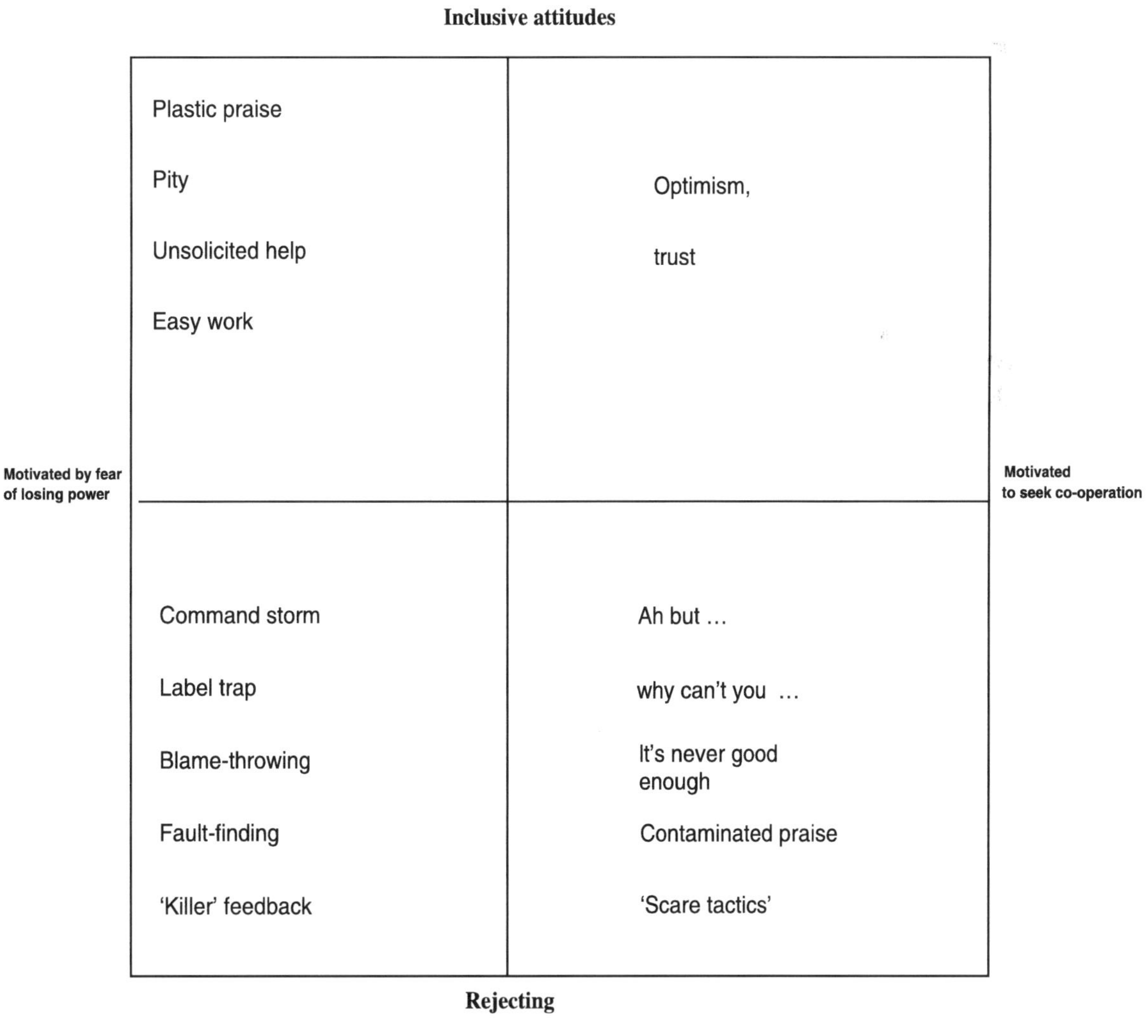

Diagram 13.1 ■ Teacher attitudes about students

In a motivating classroom, structure stresses the goals and purpose of learning rather than control. Once established, the imposition of authority should be kept to a minimum and opportunities for student initiative and autonomy maximized. For self-directed behaviour to be learned, schools need to provide the lightest of touches and the least restrictive structures necessary. Giving students leadership roles, choices and a share of responsibilities and opportunities for decision-making will foster active participation and a sense of ownership in the learning process. Optimal motivation requires stimulation through activities that involve achievable and appropriate goals, and challenge skill level, while permitting control.

The classroom drivers are overlapping. They are mutually dependent upon each other and interact in a multiplicative way. Ideally all the features work in concert and are directed towards the same outcomes. High-impact teachers use each of the four drivers and their four gears skilfully, selecting the right gear for each driver for the class.

Diagram 13.2 summarizes again the four main class types and further details the forward gears of the motivating class.

The **motivating** classroom

Third gear

- more equal teacher–student relationship
- creative learning
- flow
- critical investigation
- personal success emphasized
- self-evaluation encouraged
- students apply own criteria for progress
- feedback an integral part of class life
- student initiative maximized
- students are known well and understood
- students are autonomous learners

Second gear

- a responsive climate
- a sense of being known/valued
- a climate of self-improvement
- trust with accountability
- autonomy within structure
- constructive learning
- emphasizes personal success

First gear

- conditional acceptance, correction
- descriptive feedback
- external rewards and punishments
- receptive learning
- authoritative structure
- consistency
- clarity of purpose and goals

The **undemanding** classroom

- an overprotective climate
- a restrictive climate
- a permissive structure
- an undemanding curriculum
- praise for easy work
- pity for failure
- low expectations

The **destructive** classroom

- low expectations
- oppressive structure
- forced learning
- personal blame
- 'plastic' praise
- intimidation

The **exposing** classroom

- a competitive climate
- a 'prove yourself' climate
- high evaluative threat
- uncertainty
- chaotic structure
- unclear goals
- contaminated praise

Diagram 13.2 ■ The main class types and gears of the motivating class

Confidence-building schools operate in top gear as much as possible to instil the beliefs that ability is not fixed and that there are many ways to succeed. They portray skill development as incremental and domain specific, and hard work as a worthwhile and essential investment. They encourage students to think about how they are smart, as opposed to how smart they are, and to make optimistic attributions for success. Motivating teachers avoid the tendency to load their reactions with approval or disapproval and downplay their evaluative role by letting students evaluate themselves as much as possible (Hargreaves, 1972). They treat mistakes as essential steps to competency by linking failure to factors that students can repair.

Confidence depends less on actual achievement than on the relationship between achievement and aspirations. Effective teachers encourage an accurate match between students' aspirations and their current skills level. They praise student effort and strategy use to help students focus on the process of their work, make them feel responsible for success and emphasize the possibility of improvement. Most importantly they stress personal improvement rather than normative success.

There is a reciprocal relationship between student involvement and teacher behaviour, mediated by teacher perceptions of student motivation. Reciprocal effects often tend to magnify student's initial levels of involvement. Teachers naturally respond to motivated students with more engagement, autonomy support and positive feedback, and to demotivated students with more hostility or neglect, coercion and negative feedback.

Teachers' own motivation mindsets are 'downloaded' to students through their classroom drivers. For example, teacher beliefs about the nature of ability will lead to either a mastery or performance climate.

☐ Conclusions

Motivation can only be understood within specific learning contexts. Students can be motivated not to attempt a task as strongly as to complete it. They can be motivated in different directions, some of which may be pro- or anti-school, or they can be overmotivated for the wrong reasons. A student's motivational style can be adaptive or unhelpful.

Schools should be sceptical of any programme that offers to solve their students' motivational problems with a simple system. Evaluating one's own or a student's motivation along a single dimension is like casting a vote in a general election – a single indicator of a multiplicity of factors. Teachers need to be active decision-makers and use different kinds of information about students to make informed choices about what they need to nurture their self-motivation. Motivational strategies will be most effective when they are woven into the fabric of classroom practice and school policies. There is no fixed formula to produce self-motivated students and there will be a wide range of individual styles, but the teacher will have to have skills in each of the four drivers.

Each student is unique and all methods will not work with all individuals. Motivating teaching is characterized by the capacity to respond with sensitivity to the needs of the individual student and to invite each student to give of his or her best. A recurring theme of this book has been the need for teachers to be reflective practitioners, constantly seeking the balance between overprotection and excessive pressure, and between overcontrol and excessive freedom.

Some students do not reach anywhere near their teachers' expectations, while others of similar ability achieve more than predicted. The crucial factor that separates these groups is their motivational mindsets, especially their self-efficacy beliefs and, in particular, their ability to cope with challenges and setbacks.

Successful students have a capacity to work very hard and show a determined single-mindedness and strong commitment to their activities. They enjoy high intrinsic motivation and are deeply absorbed in their activities. They are sure about what they want to do and have a clear and strong sense of control and direction. They are free from any feelings of inferiority, are able to keep persisting however frustrating the task and so, crucially, cope well with failure and setbacks. They are high in self-efficacy beliefs.

Students with poor motivation are a heterogeneous group. They all, however, have a complex set of negative ideas about themselves as learners and disaffiliate themselves from learning. They may have low self-competence belief and little need for achievement. They may be driven by a fear of failure and have accepted a passive helplessness or developed more proactive self-protection strategies. Having a performance attitude to achievement and beliefs about the fixed nature of their ability may exacerbate these features. Demotivation is predicted by a combination of fixed-ability ideas and low-competence beliefs. Disengaged students feel they are not in control of any aspect of the learning situation. Support will most effectively be focused on specific aspects of self-efficacy rather than vague and general attempts to make students feel good about themselves.

Some students take longer than others to reach the stage of motivational maturity. Unfortunately, some schools operate like conveyor belts or assembly lines that do not accommodate different rates of progress in motivational maturity. Some students who lead difficult lives are not ready for the demands and expectations of their chronological stage. When they try to stay where they are on the school assembly line they cause disruption to school processes. These students would benefit from transitional space in which to mature at their own individual pace.

For some students, it is difficult to find any starting point to re-engage them in learning. It is like looking for the start of a roll of sticky tape. All students, however, can rediscover an interest in learning, no matter how disengaged they have become. Alternative approaches to foster learning are required that build upon the beliefs, goals, 'real-life' challenges and experiences of individuals, rather than imposing learning on the seemingly reluctant (Taylor and Cameron, 2002).

The search for a 'revitalizer' that will rekindle the motivation mindsets of such students may need to be within a new medium. Outward bound, for example, can provide novel challenges, intense relationships, close group identity, trust and the discovery of unrealized strengths (Ewert, 1989; Hogan, 1968). Drama can also provide a powerful medium to engage disaffected students by putting them on stage and letting them be the star of the show. Through peer affirmation and high-energy situations that offer trust and intimacy, drama can provide students with an emotional security and a voice to express their feelings (Quibell, 1999). In a similar way, dance releases endorphins, gets the heart rate up, promotes energy and, so, creates the bodies' natural high. Enterprise education is another example of a revitalizing learning experience with immediate attraction, because of its real-life connections. These activities and learning contexts provide different motivation drivers to draw disengaged students out of reverse gear. Schools will need to look beyond their walls for partnership to offer a relevant curriculum for all of their students' needs (Mannion, 2002).

Communication technology can be particularly helpful and is readily available. In terms of engagement, computers provide a competitive but private, therefore low-threat, climate. Engagement is unconditional. Stimulation is provided through small achievable targets. Computers offer high levels of challenge, novelty and fantasy. They allow pupils to be less reliant on teacher expertise. The structure they provide is one where the student is in full control. Perhaps most significantly, computers offer feedback that is not only instant and individualized, but is consistent, objective and, most importantly, non-judgemental.

The view that non-participation in learning is the fault of the disengaged is further alienating and less than unhelpful. Mainstream schooling can often impose learning upon passive students. The pressure on schools to produce higher and higher standards carries the risk that teachers become controlled by, rather than in control of, the curriculum. Pressure to meet targets will be downloaded to students through overcontrolling classrooms. The achievement agenda might also give the high moral ground to those academically focused teachers who teach their subjects rather than students. Some aspects of schooling may actually be working against helping students to motivate themselves.

Disengaged students need alternative learning contexts that start from, and build on, their interests and goals. Learning needs to be connected to students' lives, involving real-life challenges and experiences, rather than imposed upon the seemingly reluctant. The starting point should be what interests and will engage different groups. Learning contexts need to provide as few obstacles and threats as possible and, instead, play to students' strengths and interests and give purpose to their learning. Any learning context for those who are demotivated by the more formal culture needs to be connected to something that attracts them and links with their own subculture.

We usually think of boosting self-esteem as the way to produce confident and motivated students. Schools, however, cannot actually influence esteem as much as we think. It may indeed be the case that teachers can more readily damage self-esteem than build it, particularly for students who come to school with already vulnerable esteem. Like trust, self-esteem takes a long time to build but can be demolished very quickly. Fortunately, it is not difficult for teachers to avoid damaging student self-esteem by minimizing such destructive processes as judgemental criticism and fault-finding, personalized blame-throwing, public humiliation, capricious, overcontrolling or unfair discipline, and neglect and disinterest.

Low self-esteem is not as big a barrier to confident learning as we think. The positive conclusion drawn is that schools can readily impact on the malleable mindsets that, in turn, help nurture student self-esteem. The best strategy will be to put students in the driver seat and help them to learn how to boost their own self-esteem. Teachers are more likely to become agents of change when they recognize the agency of their students (Nixon, Walker and Barron, 2002).

Most teachers will have been attracted to teaching by the stimulation driver. Descriptions of intrinsic motivation certainly dominate discussions with teachers about their own motivating experiences (McLean, 2003). Structure has always been a priority, given that schools need to control large numbers of students. These empowerment drivers alone, however, will not be motivating without the human energy provided by the relationship drivers. Affirmation is the fuel without which the school will not nurture self-motivated students.

The single biggest learning tool in any organization is conversation (Senge *et al.*, 1994). Students need to know they count before they see any point in putting in any effort to learn. One of the problems that teachers have is finding time for the engagement driver, particularly for listening to students. Yet few things are more motivating to students than personal attention from teachers who 'seek to understand before being understood' (Covey, 1990). It is the best way of communicating the message that each student matters. Doing that is stimulating in itself, but it may also help teachers understand and work with the natural 'grain' of students' motives.

The relational aspects, particularly the relationship between students and teachers, will always be the most important aspects of schooling. Teachers increasingly will lead through their relationships with, rather than authority over, students. The feedback driver is possibly the most important driver schools have to impact on students' mindsets, yet it is the one that is perhaps the least developed. Time needs to be found for this and teachers need to be encouraged to focus on teaching students rather than subjects.

Bibliography

Abramson, L.Y., Metalsky, G.I. and Alloy, L.B. (1989) Hopelessness depression: a theory-based subtype of depression, *Psychological Review*, 96, 358–72.

Ames, C. (1992) Classrooms: goals, structures and student motivation, *Journal of Educational Psychology*, 84, 261–71.

Ames, C. and Archer, T. (1987) Mothers beliefs about the role of ability and effort in schooling, *Journal of Educational Psychology*, 79, 409–14.

Ames, C. and Archer, T. (1988) Achievement goals in the classroom, *Journal of Educational Psychology*, 80, 260–7.

Anderson, E.M. and Maehr, M.L. (1994) Motivation and schooling in the middle grades, *Review of Educational Research*, 64 (2) 287–309.

Askew, S. and Lodge, C. (2000) Gifts, ping-pong and loops – linking feedback and learning, in S. Askew (ed.), *Feedback for Learning*. London: Routledge/Falmer.

Askew, S. (2000) Communication between school and parents: correction, consultation or conversations for learning, in S. Askew (ed.), *Feedback for Learning*. London: Routledge/Falmer.

Atkinson, J. (1964) *An Introduction to Motivation*. Princeton, NJ: Van Nostrand.

Atkinson, J. and Raynor, J. (eds.) (1978) *Personality, Motivation and Achievement*. Washington, DC: Hemisphere.

Baldwin, M.A. and Sinclair, L. (1996) Self esteem and 'if ... then' contingencies of inter-personal acceptance, *Journal of Personality and Social Psychology*, 71, 1130–41.

Bandura, A. (1989) Human agency in social cognitive theory, *American Psychologist*, 44 (9), 1175–84.

Bandura, A. (1997) *Self-Efficacy The Exercise of Control*. New York: W.H. Freeman.

Barron, K.B. and Harackiewicz, J.M. (2000) Achievement goals and optimal motivation: a multiple goals approach, in C. Sanstone and J.M. Harackiewicz (eds), *Intrinsic and Extrinsic Motivation: The search for optimal motivation and performance*. New York: Academic Press.

Bartholemew, K. and Horowitz, L.M. (1991) Attachment styles among young adults, *Journal of Personality and Social Psychology*, 61, 226–44.

Baumeister, R.F. (ed.) (1993) *Self-Esteem: The Puzzle of Low Self-regard*. New York: Plenum Press.

Baumeister, R.F. and Leary, M.R. (1995) The need to belong: desire for interpersonal attachments as a fundamental human motivation, *Psychological Bulletin*, 117, 497–529.

Baumeister, R.F., Heatherton, T.F. and Rice, D.M. (1993) When ego threats lead to self-regulation failure: the negative consequences of high esteem, *Journal of Personality and Social Psychology*, 64, 141 – 56.

Baumeister, R.F., Smart, L. and Boden, J.M. (1996) Relation of threatened egotism to violence and aggression: the dark side of self-esteem, *Psychological Review*, 103 (1), 5–33.

Baumrind, D. (1991) Effective parenting during the early adolescent transition, in P.E. Cowan and E.M. Hetherington (eds), *Advances in Family Research*, vol. 2, pp. 111–63. Hillsdale, NJ: Erlbaum.

Berglas, S. (1985) Self-handicapping and self-handicappers: a cognitive/attributional model of interpersonal self-protective behaviour, in R. Hogan and W. H. Jones (eds), *Perspectives in personality*, vol. 1, pp. 235–70). Greenwich, CT: JAI Press.

Beyer, S. (1990) Gender differences in the accuracy of grade expectations and evaluations, *Sex Roles*, 41, 279–96.

Beyer, S. (1999) Gender differences in the accuracy of self-evaluations of performance, *Journal of Personality and Social Psychology*, 59, 960–70.

Biddle, S.J.H. (1977) Cognitive theories of motivation and the physical self, in K.R. Fox (ed.), *The Physical Self: From Motivation to Well-Being*. London: Human Kinetics.

Biddle, S.J.H., Fox, K.R. and Boutcher, S.H. (2000) *Physical Activity and Psychological Well Being*. London: Routledge.

Black, P. and Williams, D. (2002) *Inside the Black Box*. London: Educational Resource Centre.

Boaler, J. (1997) Setting, social class and the survival of the quickest, *British Educational Research Journal*, 23, 575–95.

Boaler, J., William, D. and Brown, M. (2000) Experiences of ability grouping – disaffection, polarisation and the construction of failure, *British Educational Research Journal*, 28 (5), 631–48.

Boggiano, A.K.and Pittman, T.S. (1992) *Achievement and Motivation: A Social Developmental Perspective*. Cambridge: Cambridge University Press.

Boggiano, A.K., Barrett, M., Weiher, A.W., McClelland, G.H., and Lusk, C.M. (1987) Use of the maximal-operant principle to motivate children's intrinsic interest, *Journal of Personality and Social Psychology*, 53, 866–79.

Boggiano, A.K., Main D.S., and Katz, P.A. (1988) Children's preference for challenge: the role of perceived competence and control, *Journal of Personality and Social Psychology*, 54, 134–41.

Braithwaite, J. (1989) *Crime, Shame, and Reintegration*. Cambridge: Cambridge University Press.

Braithwaite, J. (2001) *Restorative Justice and Responsive Regulation*. New York: Oxford University Press.

Brewer, M.B. (1991) The social self: on being the same and different at the same time, *Personality and Social Psychology Bulletin*, 17, 475–82.

Brophy, E. and Good, T.J. (1970) Teacher communication of differential expectations for children's performance, *Journal of Educational Psychology*, 61, 365–74.

Brophy, J. (1981) Teacher praise: a functional analysis, *Review of Educational Research*, 51, 5–32.

Brophy, J., and McCaslin, M. (1992) Teachers' reports of how they perceive and cope with problem students, *Elementary School Journal*, 93, 3–68.

Brown, J.D. (1993) Self-esteem and self-evaluations: feeling is believing, in J. Suls (ed.). *Psychological Perspectives on the Self*. vol. 4. Hillsdale, NJ: Erlbaum.

Brown, J.D. and McGill, K.L. (1989) The cost of good fortune: when positive life events produce negative health consequences, *Journal of Personality and Social Psychology*, 57, 1103–10.

Brown, S. (1988) *Treating Adult Children of Alcoholics: A Developmental Perspective*. New York: Wiley.

Bruner, J.S. (1983) *Child's Talk: Learning to use Language*. Oxford: Oxford University Press.

Bruner, J.S. (1996) *The Culture of Education*. Cambridge, MA: Harvard University Press.

Bugental, D.B. *et al.* (1999) Children 'tune out' in response to the ambiguous communication style of powerless adults, *Child Development,* 70 (1),.214–30.

Bull, P. (2002) *Communication under the Microscope: The Theory and Practice of Microanalysis*. London: Psychology Press.

Burger, J.M. (1990) Desire for control and interpersonal interaction style, *Journal of Research in Personality*, 24, 32–44.

Burger, J.M. (1992) *Desire for Control: Personality, Social and Clinical Perspectives*. New York: Plenum Press.

Burhans, K. and Dweck, C.S. (1995) Helplessness in early childhood: the role of contingent worth, *Child Development*, 66, 1719–38.

Burka, J.B.and Yuen, L.M. (1983) *Procrastination: Why You Do It, What to Do about It*. Reading, MA: Addison-Wesley.

Burns, D. (1993) *10 Days to Great Self-esteem*. London: Vermilion.

Burns. J.M. (1978) *Leadership*. New York: Harper and Row.

Bushman, B.J. and Baumeister, R.F. (1998) Threatened egotism, narcissism, self-esteem, and direct and displaced aggression: does self-love or self-hate lead to violence? *Journal of Personality and Social Psychology*, 75, 219–29.

Butler, R. and Nisan, M. (1986) Effects of no feedback, task-related comments, and grades on intrinsic motivation and performance, *Journal of Educational Psychology*, 78, 210–16.

Cameron, J. and Pierce, W.D. (1994) Reinforcement, reward and intrinsic motivation: a meta-analysis, *Review of Education Research*, 64, 363–423.

Cameron, J. and Pierce, W.D. (1996) The debate about rewards and intrinsic motivation: protests and accusations do not alter the results, *Review of Educational Research*, 66, 39–51.

Carver, S.C. and Scheier, M.F. (1998) *On the Self-Regulation of Behaviour*. Cambridge: Cambridge University Press.

Cassidy, J. and Asher, S.R. (1992) Loneliness and peer relations in young children, *Child Development*, 63, 350–65.

Chiu, C., Hong, Y. and Dweck, C.S. (1997) Lay dispositionism and implicit theories of personality, *Journal of Personality and Social Psychology*, 73, 923–40.

Clifford, M. (1984) Thoughts on a theory of constructive failure, *Educational Psychologist*, 19, 108–20.

Cooley, C.H. (1902) *Human Nature and the Social Order*. New York: Scribner.

Cooper, P. and McIntyre, D. (1996) *Effective Teaching and Learning: Teachers' and Students' Perspectives*. Buckingham: Open University Press.

Coopersmith, S. (1967) *The Antecedents of Self-esteem*. San Francisco, CA: Freeman.

Covey, S. (1990) *Seven Habits of Highly Effective People*. New York: Simon and Schuster.

Covington, M.V. (1998) *The Will to Learn: A Guide for Motivating Young People*. Cambridge: Cambridge University Press.

Covington, M.V. (1992) *Making the Grade: A Self Worth Perspective on Motivation and School Reform*. New York: Oxford University Press.

Covington, M.V. and Omelich, C.L. (1979) *Effort: the double-edged sword in school achievement*, Journal of Educational Psychology, 77, 446–59.

Covington, M.V. and Omelich, C.L. (1987) 'I knew it cold before the exam': a test of the anxiety blockage hypothesis, *Journal of Educational Psychology*, 79, 393–400.

Cowen, E.L. *et al.* (1973) Long term follow-up of early detected vulnerable children, *Journal of Consulting and Clinical Psychology*, 41, 438–46.

Coyne, J.C.and Lazarus, R.S. (1980) Cognitive style, stress perception, and coping, in I.L. Kutash and L.B. Schlesinger (eds), *Handbook on Stress and Anxiety*. San Francisco, CA: Jossey-Bass.

Craske, M.L. (1988) Learned helplessness: self worth motivation and attribution retraining for primary school children, *British Journal of Educational Psychology*, 58, 154–64.

Crocker, J. and Major, B. (1989) Social stigma and self-esteem: the self-protective properties of stigma, *Psychological Review*, 96, 608–30.

Crocker, J. and Luhtonen, R. (1990) Collective self-esteem and in-group bias, *Journal of Personality and Social Psychology*, 58, 60–7.

Crocker, J. and Wolfe, C. (2001) Contingencies of worth, *Psychological Review*, 108 (3), 593–623.

Cross, S.E. and Madson, L. (1997) Models of the self: self-construals and gender, *Psychological Bulletin*, 122 (1), 5–37.

Csikszentmihalyi, M. (1990) *Flow: The Psychology of Optimal Experience*. New York: Harper Perennial.

Damon, W. (1995) *Greater Expectations: Overcoming the Culture of Indulgence in America's Homes and Schools*. New York: Free Press.

Davids, A. and Hainsworth, P.K. (1967) Maternal attitudes about family life and child rearing as avowed by mothers and perceived by their under-achieving and high-achieving sons, *Journal of Consulting Psychology*, 31, 29–37.

Davidson, R.J., Putnam, K.M. and Larsen, C.L. (2000) Emotions, plasticity, context and regulation: perspectives from affective neuroscience, *Psychological Bulletin*, 126 (6), 890–909.

de Charms, R. (1968) *Personal Causation: The Internal Affective Determinants of Behaviour*. New York: Academic Press.

De Volder, M. and Lens, W. (1982) Academic achievement and future time perspective as a cognitive–motivational concept, *Journal of Personality and Social Psychology*, 42, 566–71.

Deci, E.L. (1975) *Intrinsic Motivation*. New York, Plenum Press.

Deci, E.L. and Ryan, R.M. (1985) *Intrinsic Motivation and Self-Determination in Human Behaviour*. New York: Plenum Press.

Deci, E.L. and Ryan, R.M. (1987) The support of autonomy and the control of behaviour, *Journal of Personality and Social Psychology*, 53, 1024–1037.

Deci, E.L. and Ryan, R.M. (1995) Human autonomy: The basis for true self-esteem in M.H. Kernis, (ed) *Efficacy, Agency and Self Esteem*. New York: Plenum Press.

Deci, E.L. and Ryan, R.M. (2000) Self-determination theory and the facilitation of intrinsic motivation, social development and well being, *American Psychologist,* 55.(1), 68–78.

Department for Education and Employment (1996) *Education Act 1997*. London: HMSO.

Department of Education and Science (DES) (1989) *Discipline in Schools. Report of the Committee of Inquiry*. The Elton Report. London: HMSO.

Dewey, J. (1938) *Experience and Education*. New York: Simon and Schuster.

Diene, C. and Dweck, C. (1980) An analysis of learned helplessness: II. The processing of success, *Journal of Personality and Social Psychology*, 39, 940–52.

Dornbusch, S.M., Ritter, P.L., Leiderman, P.H., Roberts, D.F. and Fraleigh, M.J. (1987) The relation of parenting style to adolescent school performance, *Child Development*, 58, 1244–57.

Duda, J.L. (1992) Dimensions of achievement motivation in schoolwork and sport, *Journal of Educational Psychology*, 84, 290–9.

Dweck, C.S. and Bush, E.S. (1976) Sex differencies on learned helplessness, *Developmental Psychology*, 12, 147–56.

Dweck, C.S. (1992) The study of goals in psychology, *Psychological Science*, 3 (3), 165–7.

Dweck, C.S. (2000) Self-theories: their role in motivation, personality and development, *Psychology Press*, Philadelphia, PA: Taylor and Francis.

Dweck, C.S. and Sorich, L. (1999) Mastery orientated thinking, in C.R. Snyder (ed.), *Coping*. New York: Oxford University Press.

Dweck, C.S. *et al.* (1988) A social-cognitive approach to motivation and personality, *Psychological Review*, 95, 256–73.

Dweck, C.S. *et al.* (1978) Sex differences in learned helplessness: the contingencies of evaluative feedback in the classroom, *Developmental Psychology*, 14, 268–76.

Dykman, B.M. (1998) Integrating cognitive and motivational factors in depression: initial tests of a goal-orientation approach, *Journal of Personality and Social Psychology*, 74, 139–58.

Eccles, J.S., Wigfield, A. and Schiefele, U. (1998) Motivation to succeed, in W. Damon and N. Eisenberg (eds), *Handbook of Child Psychology,* vol. 3. New York: Wiley.

Eccles, J.S., Buchanan, C.M., Flanagan, C., Fuligni, A., Midgley, C. and Yee, D. (1991) Control versus autonomy during early adolescence, *Journal of Social Issues*, 47, 53–68.

Eley Associates (2001) The collaboration for high performance schools, *Best Practice Manual*. www.chps.net

Elliot, A.J. and Harackiewicz, J.M. (1996) Approach and avoidance achievement goals and intrinsic motivation: a mediational analysis, *Journal of Personality and Social Psychology*, 70, 461–75.

Elliot, J.E. and Church, M.A. (1977) A hierarchical model of approach and avoidance achievement motivation, *Journal of Personality and Social Psychology*, 72 (1), 218–32.

Emler, N. (2002) *Self-esteem: The Costs and Causes of Low Self-worth*. Joseph Rowntree Trust, published by YPS.

Epstein, S. (1992) Coping ability, negative self-evaluation, and over-generalisation: experiment and theory, *Journal of Personality and Social Psychology*, 62, 826–36.

Erdley, C.S. and Dweck, C.S. (1993) Children's implicit theories as predictors of their social judgments, *Child Development*, 64, 863–78.

Etangl, C. and Harlow, H. (1975) Behaviour of male and female teachers in relation to behaviour and attitudes of elementary school children, *Journal of Genetic Psychology*, 127,

163–70.

Etzioni, A. (1996) *The responsive community: a communitarian perspective, American Sociological Review*, 61, 1–11.

Ewert, A.W. (1989) *Outdoor Adventures Pursuits: Foundations, Models and Theories*. Columbus, OH: Publishing Horizons.

Fenigstein, A. and Vanable, P.A. (1992) Paranoia and self-consciousness, *Journal of Personality and Social Psychology*, 62, 129–38.

Feiring, C. and Taska, L.S. (1996) Family self-concept: ideas on its meaning, in B. Braken (ed.), *Handbook of Self-concept*. New York: Wiley.

Ferrari, J.R., Johnson, J.L. and McCown, W.G. (1995) *Procrastination and Task Avoidance: Theory Research, and Treatment*. New York: Plenum Press.

Feuerstein, R. (1980) *Instrumental Enrichment: An Intervention Programme for Cognitive Modifiability*. Glenview, IL: Scott, Foresman.

Freire, P. (1970) *The Pedagogy of the Oppressed*. New York: Continuum.

Gabriel, S. and Gardner, W.L. (1999) Are there 'his' or 'hers' types of Interdependence? The Implications of gender differences in collective versus relational interdependence for affect, behaviour and cognition, *Journal of Personality and Social Psychology*, 77 (3), 642–55.

Galvin, P., Miller, J. and Nash, J. (1999) *Behaviour and Discipline in Schools*. London: Fulton.

Gibbons, F.X. and McCoy, S.B. (1991) Self-esteem, similarity, and reactions to active versus passive downward comparison, *Journal of Personality and Social Psychology*, 60, 414–24.

Gilligan, R. (2001) Promoting positive outcomes for children in need: the assessment of protective factors, in J. Horwath (ed.), *The Child's World: Assessing Children in Need*. London: Kingsley.

Goleman, D. (1995) *Emotional Intelligence*. New York: Bantam.

Gollwitzer, P.M. and Bargh, J.A. (1996) *The Psychology of Action Linking Cognition and Motivation to Behaviour*. New York: Guilford.

Goodnow, J.J. and Collins, W.A. (1990) *Development According to Parents: The Nature, Sources, and Consequences of Parents' Ideas*. Hillsdale, NJ: Erlbaum.

Gottfried, A. (1994) Role of parental motivational practices in children's academic intrinsic motivation and achievement, *Journal of Educational Psychology*, 86, 104–13.

Graham, S. and Barker, G.P. (1990) The down side of help: an attributional–developmental analysis of helping behaviour as a low-ability cue, *Journal of Educational Psychology*, 82, 7–14.

Grundy, S. (1987) *Curriculum Product or Praxis*. London: Falmer Press.

Hanko, G. (1994) Discouraged children: when praise does not help, *British Journal of Special Education*, 21 (4), 166–8.

Hargreaves, D. (1972) *Interpersonal Relations and Education*. London: Routledge and Kegan Paul.

Hargreaves, D. (1975) *Deviance in Classrooms*. London: Routledge and Kegan Paul.

Hart, D., Fegley, S. and Brengelman, D. (1993) Perceptions of past, present and future selves among children and adolescents, *British Journal of Developmental Psychology*, 11, 265–82.

Harter, S. (1983) Developmental perspectives on self-esteem, in P.H. Mussen (ed.), *Handbook of child psychology. Vol. IV: Socialisation, Personality, and Social Development*. New York: Wiley.

Hay Group (2000) *Research into Head Teacher Effectiveness for the Department of Education and Employment*. London: Hay Group.

Haywood, H.C. (1993) A mediational teaching style, *International Journal of Cognitive Education and Mediated Learning*, 3 (1), 32–40.

Herzberg, F., Mausner, G. and Synderman, B. (1959) *Motivation to Work*. New York: Wiley.

Higgins, E.T. (1987) Self-discrepancy: A theory relating to self and affect, *Psychological Review*, 94, 319–40.

Higgins, E.T. (1989) Self-discrepancy theory: what patterns of self-beliefs cause people to suffer?, in L. Berkowitz (ed.), *Advances in Experimental Social Psychology*, 22, 93–136. New York: Academic Press.

Higgins, E.T. (1991) Development of self-regulatory and self-evaluative processes: costs, benefits, and tradeoffs, in M.R. Gunnar and L.A. Sroufe (eds), *Self processes and development: The Minnesota symposia on child psychology*, 23, 125–65. Hillside, NJ: Erlbaum.

Higgins, E.T. and Silberman, I. (1998) Development of regulatory focus: promotion and prevention as ways of living, in J. Heckhausen and C.S. Dweck (eds), *Motivation and Self-regulation across the Life Span*. New York: Cambridge University Press.

Higgins, R.L., Snyder, C.R. and Berglas, S. (eds) (1990) *Self-handicapping: The Paradox that Isn't*. New York: Plenum Press.

Hogan, J.M. (1968) *Impelled into Experiences: The Story of the Outward Bound Schools*. Wakefield: Educational Productions.

Hoge, D., Smit, E. and Crist, J. (1995) Reciprocal effects of self-concept and academic achievement in sixth and seventh grade, *Journal of Youth and Adolescence*, 24, 295–314.

Hong, Y. *et al.* (1999) Implicit theories, attributions and coping: a meaning system approach, *Journal of Personality and Social Psychology*, 77, (3), 588–99.

Hong, Y.Y., Chiu, C. and Dweck, C.S. (1995) Implicit theories of intelligence: reconsidering the role of confidence in achievement motivation, in M.H. Kernis (ed.), *Efficacy, Agency and Self-esteem*. New York: Plenum Press.

Howe, M.J.A. (1999) *The Psychology of High Abilities*. London: Macmillan.

Hughes, J., Cavell, T. and Grossman, P. (1997) A positive view of self: risk or protection for aggressive children?, *Development and Psychopathology*, 9, 75–94.

Ireson, J. and Hallam, S. (2001) *Ability Grouping in Education*. London: Sage Publications.

Jacobs, E.J. and Eccles, J.S. (2000) *Parents, task values and real-life achievement-related choices*, in C. Sandstone and J.M. Harackiewicz (eds), *Intrinsic and Extrinsic Motivation: The Search for Optimal Motivation and Performance*. New York: Academic Press.

James, W. (1950) *The Principles of Psychology*. New York: Dover. (Original work published in 1890.)

Johnson, B.M, Shulman, S. and Collins, W.A. (1991) Systematic patterns of parenting as reported by adolescents: developmental differences and implications for psychosocial outcomes, *Journal of Adolescent Research*, 6, 235–52.

Jussim, L. (1989) Teacher expectations: self-fulfilling prophecies, perceptual biases, and accuracy, *Journal of Personality and Social Psychology*, 57, 469–80.

Juster, F.T. (1985) Preferences for work and leisure, in F.T. Juster and F.P. Stafford (eds), *Time, Goods and Well-being*. Ann Arbor, MI: Institute for Social Research, University of Michigan.

Juvonen, J. and Wentzel, K.R. (eds) (1996) *Social Motivation: Understanding Children's School Adjustment*. Cambridge: Cambridge University Press.

Kamins, M.L. and Dweck, C.S. (1998) Contingent self-worth and its effects on young children's coping with setbacks. Unpublished data.

Kamins, M.L. and Dweck, C. (2000) Person vs process praise and criticism: implications for contingent self-worth and coping, *Developmental Psychology*, vol. 35, (3) 835–47.

Kavussanu, M. and Harnisch, D.L. (2000) Self-esteem in children: do goal orientations matter?, *British Journal of Educational Psychology*, 70, 229–42.

Keegan, D. *et al.* (1995) Not all high (or low) self-esteem people are the same: theory and research on stability of self-esteem, in M.H. Kernis (ed.), *Efficacy, Agency and Self Esteem*. New York: Plenum Press.

Kendler, K.S., Gardner, C.O. and Prescott, C.A. (1998) A population-based twin study of self-esteem and gender, *Psychological Medicine*, 28, 1403–9.

Kennedy, W.A. and Willcutt, H.C. (1964) Praise and blame as incentives, *Psychological Bulletin*, 62, 323–32.

Kernis, M.H. (ed.) (1995) *Efficacy, Agency and Self-esteem*. New York: Plenum Press.

Kernis, M.H. and Waschull, S.B. (1996) The interactive roles of stability and level of self-esteem: research and theory, in M.P. Zanna (ed.), *Advances in Experimental Social Psychology*, vol. 27. San Diego: Academic Press.

Kernis, M.H., Cornell, D.P., Sun, C. and Berry, A. (1995) There's more to self-esteem than whether it's high or low: the importance of stability of self-esteem, *Journal of Personality and Social Psychology*, 65, 1190–204.

Kernis, M.H., Granneman, B.D. and Barclay L.C. (1989) Stability and level of self esteem as predictors of anger arousal and hostility, *Journal of Personality and Social Psychology*, 56, 1013–23.

King, K.C., Hyde, J.S. Sowers, C.J. and Buswell, B.N. (1999) Gender differences in self-esteem: a meta-analysis, *Psychological Bulletin*, 125, 470–500.

Klein, H.J. *et al.* (1999) Goal commitment and the goal setting process: conceptual clarification and empirical synthesis, *Journal of Applied Psychology* (6), 885–96.

Kohlmann, C.W., Schumacher, A. and Streit, R. (1988) Trait anxiety and parental child-rearing behaviour: support as a moderator variable?, *Anxiety Research*, 1, 53–64.

Kohn, A. (1986) *No Contest: The Case against Competition*. Boston, MA: Houghton-Mifflin.

Kounin, J. (1970) *Discipline and Group Management in Classrooms*. New York: Holt Rinehart and Winston.

Kreiman, G, Koch, C. and Fried, I. (2000) Imagery neurons in the human brain, *Nature*, 408, 357–61.

Kruglanski, A.W. and Webster, D.M. (1996) Motivated closing of the mind: 'seizing' and 'freezing', *Psychological Review*, 103, 263–83.

Kun, A. (1977) Development of the magnitude–covariation and compensation schemata in ability and effort attributions of performance, *Child Development*, 48, 862–73.

Learning and Teaching Scotland (2002) *Education for Citizenship*. Glasgow: Learning and Teaching.

Lepper, M.R. (1981) Intrinsic and extrinsic motivation in children: detrimental effects of superfluous social controls, in W.A. Collins (ed.), *Minnesota Symposia on Child Psychology*, 14, 145–214. Hillsdale, NJ: Erlbaum.

Lepper, M.R. and Henderlong, J. (2000) Turning 'play' into 'work' and 'work' into 'play': 25 years of research on intrinsic versus extrinsic motivation, in C. Sandstone and J.M. Harackiewicz (eds) *Intrinsic and Extrinsic Motivation: The Search for Optimal Motivation and Performance*. New York: Academic Press.

Lepper M.R. and Hodell, M. (1989) Intrinsic motivation in the classroom, in C. Ames and R. Ames (eds), *Research on Motivation in Education. Vol. 3: Goals and Cognition*. New York: Academic Press.

Lepper, M.R. and Henderlong, J. (1996) Intrinsic motivation and extrinsic rewards: a commentary on Cameron and Pierce's meta-analysis, *Review of Educational Research*, 66, 5–32.

Levy, S., Stroessner, S. and Dweck, C. (1998) Stereotype formation and endorsement: the role of implicit theories, *Journal of Personality and Social Psychology*, 74, 1421–36.

Lewis, T., Amini, F. and Lannon, R. (2000) *A General Theory of Love*. New York: Random House.

Licht, B. and Dweck, C. (1984) Sex differences in achievement orientations: consequences for academic choices and attainments, in M. Marland (ed.) *Sex Differentiation and Schooling*. London: Heinneman.

Lightbody, P., Siann, G., Stocks, R. and Walsh, D. (1996) Motivation and attribution in secondary school: the role of gender, *Educational Studies*, 22, 13–25.

Locke, E. and Latham, G.P. (1990) *A Theory of Goal Setting and Task Performance*. Englewood Cliffs, NJ: Prentice-Hall.

Maccoby, E.E. and Jacklin, C.N. (1974) The Psychology of sex differences. Stanford, CA: Stanford University Press.

Maccoby, E.E. and Martin, J. (1983) Socialization in the family context: parent child interaction, in E.M. Hetherington (ed.), *Handbook of Child Psychology*, vol. 4. New York: Wiley.

Maehr, M. and Midgeley, C. (1996) *Transforming School Culture*. Boulder, CO: Westview Press.

Maehr, M.L. (1991) The 'psychological environment' of the school: a focus for school leadership, in P. Thurston and P. Zodhiates (eds), *Advances in Educational Administration*, pp. 51–81. Greenwich, CT: JAI Press.

Maines, B. and Robinson, G. (1992) *The No Blame Approach*. Bristol: Lame Duck Publishing.

Maltz, D.N. and Borker, R.A. (1983) A cultural approach to male–female miscommunication, in J.D. Gumperz (ed.), *Language and Social Identity*. New York: Cambridge University Press.

Mangan, J., Adnett, N. and Davis, P. (2001) Movers and stayers: determinants of post–16 educational choice, *Research in Post Compulsory Education*, 6 (1), 31–50.

Mannion, G. (2002) Open the gates an that's it 'see ya later!' School cultures and young people's transitions into post-compulsory education and training, *Scottish Educational Review*, 34 (2), 86–100.

Markus, H. and Ruvolo, A. (1989) Possible selves: personalised representatives of goals, in L. Pervin (ed.), *Goal Concepts in Personality and Social Psychology*, pp. 211–41. Hillsdale, NJ: Erlbaum.

Maslow, A.H. (1968) *Toward a Psychology of Being*. Princeton, NJ: Van Nostrand.

Masten, A. and Coatsworth, J. (1998) The development of competencies in favourable and unfavourable environments: lessons from research on successful children, *American Psychologist*, 53 (2), 205–20.

McClelland, D. (1985) *Human Motivation*. Glenville, IL: Scott, Foresman.

McClelland, D.C. *et al.* (1980) The need for power: brain norepinephrine turnover and learning, *Biological Psychology*, 10, 93–102.

McCombs, B.L. (1993) Learner centred psychological principles for enhancing education: applications in school settings, in L.A. Penner *et al.* (eds), *The Challenge in Maths and Science Education: Psychology's Response*. Washington, DC: American Psychology Association.

McIlvanney, W. (2001) *Scotland on Sunday*, 12 March 2001.

McLean, A. (1987) After the belt: school processes in low exclusion schools, *School Organisation*, 7 (3), 303–10.

McLean, A. (1990) *Promoting Positive Behaviour in the Primary School*. Glasgow: Strathclyde Regional Council.

McLean, A. (1997) Bullyproofing Our School. Topic Issue 17 Spring 1997. NFER.

McLean, A. (2003) Exploring teachers' understanding of pupil motivation, *Educational Psychology in Scotland*, 7 (1), in press.

Merret, F. and Wheldall,T. (1990) *Positive Teaching in the Primary School*. London: Sage Publications.

Mindstore (1998) *The Learning Game*. Glasgow: Mindstore.

Minuchin, P. *et al.* (1983) The school as a context for social development, in P. Mussen and E.M. Hetherington (eds), *Handbook of Child Psychology*. New York: Wiley.

Minuchin, P.P. and Shapiro, E.K. *Handbook of Child Psychology*. 4th Edition.

Molden, D.C and Dweck, C.S. (2000) Meaning and Motivation, in C. Sandstone and J.M. Harackiewicz, *Intrinsic and Extrinsic Motivation: The Search for Optimal Motivation and Performance*. New York: Academic Press.

Mueller, C.M. and Dweck, C.S. (1996) Implicit theories of intelligence: relation of parental beliefs to children's expectations. Paper presented at the Third National Research Convention of Head Start, Washington, DC.

Mueller, C.M. and Dweck, C.S. (1998) Intelligence Praise can undermine children's motivation and performance. *Journal of Personality and Social Psychology*, 75 (1), 33–52.

Munn, P. and Lloyd, G. (2000) *Alternatives to Exclusion*. London: Sage Publications.

Nicholls, J.G., Patashnick, M. and Nolen, S.B. (1985) Adolescents' theories of education, *Journal of Educational Psychology*, 77, 683–92.

Nixon, J., Walker, M. and Barron, S. (2002) The cultural mediation of state policy: the democratic potential of new community schooling in Scotland, *Journal of Educational Policy*, 17 (4), 407–21.

Nolen-Hoeksema, S. (1990) *Sex Differences in Depression*. Stanford, CA: Stanford University Press.

Nolen-Hoeksema, S. (1995) Gender differences in coping with depression across the life span, *Depression*, 3, 81–90.

Nolen-Hoeksema, S. and Girgus, J.S. (1994) The emergence of gender differences in depression during adolescence, *Psychological Bulletin*, 115, 424–43.

Nolen-Hoeksema, S., Girgus, J.S. and Seligman, M.E.P. (1986) Learned helplessness in children: a longitudinal study of depression, achievement, and explanatory style, *Journal of Personality and Social Psychology*, 51, 435–42.

Nuttin, J. and Lens, W. (1985) *Future Time Perspective and Motivation: Theory and Research Method*. Hillsdale, NJ: Erlbaum.

Pacific Institute (2000) *Investment in Excellence*, Pacific Institute, www.pacificinstitute.co.uk

Pellegrini, A.D. and Blatchford, P. (2000) *The Child at School: Interactions with Peers and Teachers*. London: Arnold.

Peterson, C., Maier, S. and Seligman, M. (1993) *Learned Helplessness: A Theory for the Age of Personal Control*. New York: Oxford University Press.

Pikas, A. (1989) The common concern method for the treatment of mobbing, in E. Roland and E. Munthe (eds), *Bullying: An International Perspective*. London: Fulton.

Pintrich, P.R. and Schunk, D.H. (1996) *Motivation in Education Theory, Research and Application*, Englewood Cliffs, NJ: Merrill Prentice-Hall.

Pittman, T.S., Boggiano, A.K. and Ruble, D.N. (1983) Intrinsic and extrinsic motivational orientations: interactive effect of reward, competence feedback, and task complexity, in J. Levine and M. Wang (eds), *Teacher and Student Perceptions: Implications for Learning*, 319–40. Hillsdale, NJ: Erlbaum.

Pomerantz, E.M. and Ruble, D.N. (1998) The multidimensional nature of control: implications for the development of sex differences in self-evaluation, in J. Heckhausen and C.S. Dweck (eds), *Motivation and Self-regulation across the Life Span*. New York: Cambridge University Press.

Quibell, T. (ed.) (1999) *Total Learning Challenge: Action on Disaffection*. New York: TLC Publishing.

Raffini, J. (1993) *Winners without Losers: Structures and Strategies for Increasing Student Motivation to Learn*. Boston, MA: Allyn and Bacon.

Rayner, M. and Montague, M. (2000) *Resilient Children and Young People: A Discussion Paper Based on a Review of the International Research Literature*. Melbourne: Policy and Practice Research Unit, Children's Welfare Association of Victoria.

Rhodes, J. and Ajmal, Y. (1995) *Solution Focused Thinking in Schools*. London: BT Press.

Rholes, W.S., Newman, L.S. and Ruble, D.N. (1990) Understanding self and other: developmental and motivational aspects of perceiving persons in terms of invariant dispositions, in E.T. Higgins and R.M. Sorrentino (eds), *Handbook of Motivation and Cognition: Foundations of Social Behaviour*, vol 2. New York: Guilford.

Roberts, T. (1991) Gender and the Influence of evaluation on self-assessment in achievement settings, *Psychological Bulletin*, 109, 297–308.

Robertson, J. (1981) *Effective Classroom Control*. London: Hodder and Stoughton.

Roeser, R.W., Midgley, C. and Urdan, T.C. (1996) Perceptions of the school psychological environment and early adolescents' psychological and behavioural functioning in school: the mediating role of goals and belonging, *Journal of Educational Psychology*, 88, 408–22.

Rogers, B.(1991) *You Know the Fair Rule – Strategies for Making the Hard Job of Discipline in School Easier*. London: Longman.

Rogers, C.R. (1961) *On Becoming a Person*. Boston MA: Houghton Mifflin.

Rohner, R.P. (1966) *Handbook for the Study of Parental Acceptance and Rejection*. Centre for the Study of Parental Acceptance and Rejection, CT: University of Connecticut.

Rosenberg, M. (1965) *Society and the Adolescent Self-image*. Princeton, NJ: Princeton University Press.

Rosenthal, R. and Jacobsen, L. (1968) *Pygmalion in the Classroom: Teacher expectation and pupils' intellectual development*. New York: Holt, Rinehart and Winston.

Ruble, D.N. *et al.* (1993) The role of gender-related processes in the development of sex differences in self-evaluation and depression, *Journal of Affective Disorders*, 29, 97–128.

Rudduck, J. *et al.* (1998) *Sustaining Pupils' Commitment to Learning: The Challenge of Year 8*. Cambridge: Publications Unit, Homerton College.

Ryan, R.M. (1982) Control and Information in the intrapersonal sphere: an extension of the cognitive evaluation theory, *Journal of Personality and Social Psychology*, 43, 450–61.

Ryan, R.M. (1993) Agency and organisation: intrinsic motivation, autonomy and the self in psychological development, in J. Jacobs (ed.), *Nebraska Symposium on Motivation: Developmental Perspectives on Motivation*, vol. 40, 1–56. Lincoln, NE: University of Nebraska Press.

Ryan, R.M. and Deci, E.L. (2000) When rewards compete with nature: undermining of intrinsic motivation and self-regulation, in C. Sandstone and J.M. Harackiewicz (eds), *Intrinsic and Extrinsic Motivation: The Search for Optimal Motivation and Performance*. New York: Academic Press.

Ryan, R.M. and La Guardia, J.G. (1999) Achievement motivation within a pressurised society: intrinsic and extrinsic motivations to learn and the politics of school reform, in T. Urdan (ed.), *Advances in motivation and achievement*, 2, 45–86. Greenwich, CT: JAI Press.

Ryan R.M. and Powelson C.L. (1991) Autonomy and relatedness as fundamental to motivation and education, in B.L. McCombs (ed.), *Unravelling Motivation: New Perspectives from Research and Practice*. Special issue of the *Journal of Experimental Education*, Fall.

Sadler, D. (1989) Formative Assessment and the design of instructional systems, *Instructional Science*, 18, 119–44.

Sandstone, C. and Harackiewicz, J.M. (eds) (2000) I*ntrinsic and Extrinsic Motivation: The Search for Optimal Motivation and Performance*. New York: Academic Press.

SEED (2001) *Better Behaviour Better Learning – Report of the Discipline Task Force*. Edinburgh: Scottish Executive Education Department.

Seligman, M.E. (1998) *Learned Optimism*. New York: Pocket Books.

Seligman, M.E., Reivich, K., Jaycox, L. and Gilham, J. (1995) *The Optimistic Child*. Boston, MA: Houghton Mifflin.

Senge, P. *et al.* (1994) *The Fifth Discipline Fieldbook: Strategies and Tools for Building a Learning Organisation*. London: Brealey.

Shatte, A.J. *et al.* (1999) Learned optimism, in C.R. Snyder (ed.), *Coping: The Psychology of What Works*. New York: Oxford University Press.

Skinner, E.A. (1993) Motivation in the classroom: reciprocal effects of teacher behaviour and student engagement across the school year, *Journal of Educational Psychology*, 85, 571–81.

Skinner, E.A., Wellborn, J.G. and Connell, J.P. (1990) What it takes to do well in school and whether I've got it: a process model of perceived control and children's engagement and achievement in school, *Journal of Educational Psychology*, 82, 22–32.

Slavin, R.E. (1984) Students motivating students to excel: cooperative incentives, cooperative tasks, and student achievement, *Elementary School Journal*, 85, 53–64.

Snyder, C.R. (1994) *The Psychology of Hope*. New York: Free Press.

Snyder, C.R. *et al.* (1983) *Excuses: The Masquerade Solution*. New York: Wiley.

Stipek, D.J. (1995) The development of pride and shame in toddlers, in J.P. Tangney and K. W. Fischer (eds), *Self-conscious emotions: The Psychology of Shame, Guilt, Embarrassment, and Pride*. New York: Guilford.

Stipek, D.J., Rechia, S. and McLintic, S. (1992) Self-evaluation in young children. Monographs of the Society for Research in Child Development, 57 (226).

Swann, W.B. (1996) *Self Traps: The Elusive Quest for Higher Self Esteem*. New York: Freeman.

Swann, W.B., Pelham, B.W. and Krull, D.S. (1989) Agreeable fancy or disagreeable truth? Reconciling self-enhancement and self-verification, *Journal of Personality and Social Psychology*, 57, 782–91.

Tangney, J.P. (1995) Shame and guilt in interpersonal relationships, in J.P. Tangney and K.W. Fischer (eds), *Self-conscious Emotions: The Psychology of Shame, Guilt, Embarrassment and Pride*. New York: Guilford.

Taylor, S. and Cameron, H. (eds) (2002) *Attracting New Learners – International Evidence and Practice*. London: Learning and Skills Developing Agency.

Taylor, S.E. (1990) *Positive Illusions: Creative Self-deception and the Healthy Mind*. New York: Basic Books.

Terdal, S. and Leary, M.R. (1991) Social exclusions, self-esteem and dysphoria. Paper presented at the meeting of the South Eastern Psychological Association, New Orleans.

Thompson, T. (1999) *Underachieving to Protect Self-worth: Theory, Research and Interventions.* Aldershot: Ashgate.

Tuckman, B.W. and Sexton, T.L. (1990) The relation between self-beliefs and self-regulated performance, *Journal of Social Behaviour and Personality,* 5, 465–72.

Tuckman, B.W. (1995) *Teaching Children How to Succeed.* Elizabethtown, PA: Continental Press.

Tyler, T.R., Kramer, R.M. and John, P.J. (eds) (1998) *The Psychology of the Social Self.* New York: Erlbaum.

Vallerand, R.J., Guay, F. and Fortier, M.J. (1997) Self-determination and persistence in a real-life setting: towards a motivational model of high school drop out. *Journal of Personality and Social Psychology,* 72 (5), 1161–72.

Van Wersch, A. (1997) Individual differences and intrinsic motivations for sports participation, in J. Kremer (ed.), *Young People's Involvement in Sport.* London: Routledge.

Vygotsky, l.S. (1978) *Mind in Society.* Cambridge, MA: Harvard University Press.

Weiner, B. (ed.) (1974) *Achievement Motivation and Attribution Theory.* Morris-town, NJ: General Learning Press.

Weiner, B. (1986) *An Attributional Theory of Motivation and Emotion.* New York: Springer Verlag.

Weiner, B. (1992) *Human Motivation Metaphors, Theories and Research.* London: Sage.

West, M.O. and Prinz, R.J. (1987) Parental alcoholism and childhood psychopathology, *Psychological Bulletin,* 102, 204–18.

Whiting, B. and Edwards, C.P. (1973) A cross cultural analysis of sex differences in the behaviour of children aged 3 to 11, *Journal of Social Psychology,* 91, 171–88.

Wigfield, A. (1984) Expectancy–value theory of achievement motivation: a developmental perspective, *Educational Psychology Review,* 6, 49–78.

Wiggins, G. (1989) A true test: toward more authentic and equitable assessment, *Phi Delta Kappan,* 70 (9), 703–13.

Wilkins, R. and Head, M. (2002) *How to Retain and Motivate Experienced Teachers.* Canterbury: Christ Church University.

Winston, R. (2002) *The Human Instinct.* London: BBC Books.

Zimmerman, B.J. (1990) Self-regulated academic learning and achievement: the emergence of a social cognitive perspective, *Educational Psychology Review,* 2, 173–201.

Zimmerman, B.J., Bandura, A. and Martinez-Pons, M. (1992) Self-motivation for academic attainment: the role of self-efficacy beliefs and personal goal setting, *American Educational Research Journal,* 29, 663–76.

Zimmerman, B.J., Bonner, S. and Kovach, R. (1996) *Developing Self-Regulated Learners: Beyond Achievement to Self-efficacy.* Washington, DC: American Psychological Association.

Zuckerman, M., Kieffery, S.C. and Knee, C.R. (1998) Consequences of self-handicapping: effects on coping, academic performance and adjustment, *Journal of Personality and Social Psychology,* 74, 1619–28.

Index